IMAGES
of America

CHESAPEAKE BAY DECK BOATS

The deck boat *C.E. Wright* was constructed by Deltaville, Virginia, boatbuilder George Landon "Ladd" Wright in 1918. The vessel was named after Wright's newborn daughter, Countess E. Wright. Herman Thomas of Tangier Island, Virginia, is shown standing on the Samson post of the *C.E. Wright* in Crisfield, Maryland, in the 1950s. Hickman and Sterling Fish and Oyster Co. is visible in the background. (Courtesy of Newman Thomas.)

ON THE COVER: The crew of *Miss Virginia* is pictured buying oysters from hand-tong oystermen on Piankatank River. During the post–Civil War years, oysters provided economic salvation for former slaves and their descendants. African American watermen worked out of small skiffs, and many earned enough currency to buy land, homes, and bigger boats. It was hard and dangerous work. The narrow-beam skiffs ranged from 12 to 18 feet long. When a skiff was loaded down with oysters, keeping it steady in rough seas was challenging. (Courtesy of Cloyde Wiley III; photograph by Mutt Carlton.)

IMAGES of America
CHESAPEAKE BAY DECK BOATS

Larry S. Chowning

Copyright © 2020 by Larry S. Chowning
ISBN 978-1-4671-0519-4

Published by Arcadia Publishing
Charleston, South Carolina

Printed in the United States of America

Library of Congress Control Number: 2020930490

For all general information, please contact Arcadia Publishing:
Telephone 843-853-2070
Fax 843-853-0044
E-mail sales@arcadiapublishing.com
For customer service and orders:
Toll-Free 1-888-313-2665

Visit us on the Internet at www.arcadiapublishing.com

Dedicated to all of the Chesapeake Bay deck boat captains and owners who have been so dedicated to keeping the boats alive

Contents

Acknowledgments		6
Introduction		7
1.	From Sail to Power	11
2.	Log Boats	25
3.	Freight and Passenger Boats	35
4.	Buying and Planting Seed Oysters	47
5.	Oyster and Crab Dredging	59
6.	Runners and Buyboats	71
7.	Pound-Net and Haul-Seine Boats	83
8.	Pleasure and Education Boats	105
Bibliography		127

ACKNOWLEDGMENTS

I want to thank all those who have assisted me in this effort to produce a photographic history of Chesapeake Bay deck boats—without your help, this would not have been possible. I also want to thank all those who contributed to my earlier book *Chesapeake Bay Buyboats*. The book was released in 2003 and is the definitive history of the boats. Those who helped with that project inspired me to move forward with this new book. I also want to thank past and present bay historians and writers who have kept the history of the boats alive. Robert H. Burgess, Howard I. Chapelle, Tom Horton, Isabel Gough, John Frye, John Whitehead, Pete Letcher, Richard Dodds, and Paula Johnson have, in their own ways, contributed to this work. I personally want to thank William C. "Bill" Hight, John and Vera England, David Cantera, David Wright, Kevin Flynn, Ted Parrish, Edwin W. Rice, David and Trudy Rollins, Joe Conboy, Nola Watson, Jean Holman, John M. Bareford Jr., Jonesey Payne, Ray V. Rodgers III, Carroll Ashburn, Jack and Barbara Ashburn, Francis Goddard, Gretchen and Kim Granberry, and Jane Mason, who have provided photographs and encouragement over the years. I also thank the late Joseph E. Nettles, my journalism professor at the University of Richmond, who taught me the strength and significance of the written word and encouraged me to pursue a career in journalism. Finally, I want to thank my wife, Dee Chowning, who has supported me in my quest to preserve the history, heritage, and culture of Chesapeake Bay.

INTRODUCTION

Once, there were over 2,000 Chesapeake Bay deck boats on the bay. Today, there are approximately 40 left in various stages of life. Some are completely restored, while others are lying at rest in a cove or on a mudflat with the tide rising and falling inside their hulls.

The forerunners of modern deck boats were sail-powered sloops, schooners, pungies, bugeyes, and skipjacks. In the early 1900s, these boats worked many of the same jobs that would later be taken over by motorized boats. Many of these sailing craft were later converted to power, used in the bay's freight and seafood businesses, and worked right alongside the modern-style deck boat.

Chesapeake Bay mariners were excellent sailors, and during the days of sail, more commercial sailing craft plied the waters of the Chesapeake than any other waterway in the United States. Sail-driven craft were vital to the bay's economic life, as rivers and creeks and the Atlantic Coast's Intracoastal Waterway were main avenues for freighting. North Carolina, Maryland, and Virginia watermelon and vegetable trades grew from the era of sail and were eventually taken over by deck boats. Lumber, coal, fertilizer, grain, livestock, barrel staving, oysters, tomato baskets, canned vegetables, fish scrap, bricks, pig iron, and other commodities were hauled by sail and would become part of the freight business of motorized deck boats.

After the introduction of gasoline engines, many of the bay's old sailing vessels were stripped of their sails and rigging and converted to powerboats. Early sailboat-to-powerboat conversions were primitive, with bowsprits and rigging left on the boat or the bowsprit cut halfway off. These were called hybrids. Later conversions were more professional, and the old sailboats took on much the same appearance as modern deck boats.

Motor-powered deck boats often carried a single steadying, or stay, sail. When cruising in strong seas with as little as 25 horsepower, early power sources were not strong enough to keep a boat steady. A single sail was used to steady the boat as it moved through choppy seas. Steadying sails were common on deck boats until the 1940s, when developers began to create engines with enough horsepower to drive a boat through strong seas without sail assistance.

From 1910 to the 1940s, motorized deck boats were busy carriers of freight in the Chesapeake Bay region. By the 1920s, deck boats had taken over much of the freight business from sailing craft, and in that decade, more deck boats were built and sailing vessels converted to power than in any other decade. In 1932, when the Virginia General Assembly voted to take over the maintenance of the state's secondary roads, freight business began to shift away from deck boats to overland trucking. Prior to the Byrd Act, Virginia's secondary roads were made of dirt and poorly maintained, and the waterways of the Chesapeake provided a more dependable avenue for transporting freight.

As the seafood business grew on the bay, oyster-shucking and crab-picking houses, fish- and roe-canning and pickling houses, soft-shell crab shedding businesses, and various other seafood facilities provided work for deck boats. Seafood-processing plants were often some distance from rivers and creeks where watermen were working. Early on, watermen worked in small sail-driven log canoes or low-horsepower gasoline-powered boats. These boats were unsuitable for carrying heavy payloads over long distances and to the processing houses in a timely manner. Deck boat captains and crews acted as middlemen and would motor out and anchor on the fishing grounds. The deck boat crew would purchase seafood from the watermen and haul it back to the processing houses. Watermen referred to these deck boats as buyboats. Today, the term "buyboat" is used as often to identify the style of boat as "deck boat." The deck boat name, however, speaks to the fact that all deck boats have planked decks with a house/pilothouse built atop the deck and positioned near the stern. Deck boat is a more universally appropriate name, because not all deck boats were used as buyboats to purchase seafood.

The seafood industry supported a fleet of deck boats into the 1980s and 1990s. Watermen worked the boats in the oyster, finfish, and crab fisheries. In Virginia, motorized deck boats are allowed, by law, to dredge oysters on private state-leased oyster grounds. Although deck boats can be used in both Maryland and Virginia as seafood buyboats, under Maryland state law, the boats cannot be used in Maryland waters to dredge oysters. Sail- and wind-powered skipjacks are the required platform used in Maryland. The Virginia law allowing motor-powered deck boats to work on private oyster grounds greatly contributed to the popularity of deck boats in Virginia waters and to the fact that more boats were built in Virginia than in Maryland.

Deck boats were also extensively used in Virginia and Maryland pound-net and haul-seine fisheries. Haul seine and pound nets enabled fishermen to catch large quantities of fish. This created a demand for large wooden boats that could carry thousands of pounds of fish and haul heavy, awkward gear. Deck boats were the answer to this demand. The boats were also used to install pound-net poles and netting. A sturdy platform was required for fishermen to drive long, heavy pound poles into the bottoms of the bay and rivers. Many deck boats were specifically built for pound-net and haul-seine fishing.

The boats were also used to work purse nets when harvesting menhaden. Boats in that fishery are referred to as snapper rigs, a title used to differentiate between the smaller wooden deck boats and the bigger steel-hull menhaden steamers used to harvest large quantities of menhaden. The large boats catch fish that will be used to produce fish meal and oil and other high-protein supplements. The smaller snapper rigs catch fish to supply bait to lobster, crab, and eel fisheries along the East Coast.

Another element that played a role in extending the life of Chesapeake Bay deck boats was Virginia's winter crab-dredge fishery, which started at the turn of the 20th century; deck boats remained the main platform in the fishery until the 1970s and 1980s. During those decades, watermen began to work the fishery in standard deadrise hulls enlarged from 42 feet in length to 45 to 50 feet and with an increased beam that allowed two dredges to be worked off the stern. Historically, the advantage of working a deck boat in the crab-dredge fishery was the ability to haul two dredges—one off of each side. The smaller, 42-foot standard deadrises were limited to working one dredge off the stern, as they were not wide enough to accommodate two. When watermen enlarged the boats, vessels were able to be worked with two dredges off the stern, taking away that advantage from traditional deck boats. The smaller boats were less expensive to maintain and operate. Many watermen moved away from using deck boats, but a few remained in the fishery to the end. The 100-year-old crab-dredge winter fishery season was closed by the Virginia Marine Resources Commission in 2008 due to conservation concerns.

The fishery, however, saved many of the bay's deck boats that are still around today. Crab dredging gave captains and crews of the boats a way to financially support the upkeep of them. This extended the life of some deck boats into the 1970s, 1980s, and 1990s. During those decades, recreational yachtsmen, museums, and other nonprofits started buying deck boats and converting them into yachts and charter and education boats.

In the course of the life cycle of deck boats, some vessels had unique jobs. The boats *Nellie Jane* and *Lorie Robins* were used to carry groceries and goods to Tangier Island from Crisfield, Cape Charles, and Reedville. The deck boat *Island Star*, originally named *Frances*, was Maryland's school boat No. 53, used to carry children from Smith Island to high school in Crisfield. *Eleanor White* was a fuel boat used to haul gasoline from Crisfield to Tylerton and Ewell on Smith Island. The *Ruth S.* hauled Pasha, a 2,775-pound elephant belonging to Roberts Brothers Circus, to Tangier Island. The *Richmond News Leader* reported in 1977 that "the coming of Pasha and her friends has been billed as the great Chesapeake Bay elephant float."

Shortly after the Japanese invasion of Pearl Harbor in December 1941, the US government began a nationwide conscription of boats large enough to help with the war effort. Many deck boats became official federal government boats, and their captains were given rank in the "temporary reserves" of the US Coast Guard. The boats were used to patrol the region and report German U-boat sightings. Some larger boats were used for government freighting between Cuba and the

United States mainland. While it was serving as part of the coast guard fleet searching for U-boats, the deck boat *Stewart Brothers* mysteriously blew up in 1943 at the dock in Cape Charles, killing the engineer. Blame was laid on the Germans. During the war, the deck boat *Janice* was used as a fireboat in Charleston, South Carolina.

The boats ranged in size from 38 to 100 feet long. The smallest deck boats were built for the haul-seine fishery. The largest one, *Marydel*, which was over 100 feet long, was built in 1927 by Linwood Price of Deltaville and used to freight fertilizer on Chesapeake and Delaware Bays.

Some deck boats were made of logs in the tradition of log-hulled sail-powered bugeyes. The majority of the boats, however, were built with planks in traditional deadrise and cross-planked-bottom style. Some deck boats were built with the bottom planking laid longitudinal—stem to stern. The largest stem-to-stern planked deck boat, *Chesapeake*, was 100 feet long and built by Capt. Lepron "Lep" Johnson of Johnson Marine Railway in Crittenden, Virginia. She was lofted at the railway. A half-model built to scale was used to shape her hull. She was launched at midnight during the highest tide of the month to allow her seven-foot draft to float in Chuckatuck Creek.

Most deck boats were built "from rack of eye" with no official plans. The deck boats *Mobjack*, *Ocean View*, and *Marie* were built after World War II by Linwood and Milford Price and were unique in that the boats were designed by naval architect C.T. Forsberg of Freeport, New York, and built to plans.

In 2004, a group of deck boat owners from Maryland and Virginia formed the Chesapeake Bay Buyboat Association, and once a year, the owners and captains of the boats cruise to cities, towns, and villages on the bay to promote the heritage and culture of the boats. The levels of restoration are varied among these boats. Some boats are maintained in the style of commercial fishing boats, while others have undergone six-figure restoration projects and been transformed into elaborate yachts with full living accommodations.

One

FROM SAIL TO POWER

Sail-powered schooners, sloops, pungies, and bugeyes were forerunners to the modern motor-powered deck boat. Sailboats relied on God's wind and tide to travel. When nature did not provide those elements, boats laid over, costing owners, captains, and crews time and money. An engine-powered deck boat had an advantage over one with a sail because it was able to go from point A to point B within a scheduled time frame. The switch from sail to power was gentle in the beginning, as early gasoline engines were primitive and not always powerful enough to move boats at a desirable speed. Early motor-powered deck boats carried a stay, or steadying, sail, which provided some speed but mostly aided in keeping the boat steady when underway. As power increased with larger motors, the advantage of motor power became apparent. In the 1920s, more sailing vessels were converted to power and more new deck boats were built than in any other decade. The successful transition from sail to power and the successful construction evolution of the Chesapeake Bay deadrise deck boat brought an end to the bay's golden age of commercial sailboats.

This early-20th-century photograph, taken at Winegar's Marine Railway in Ocran, Virginia, shows three deck boats. One of the boats has its steadying sail up and drying. After rain or heavy dew, sails were raised at the dock to eliminate mildew and sail rot. Deck boat owners stopped using sails in the 1940s, when internal combustion engines were powerful enough to drive the boats through strong seas without the need for a steadying sail. (Courtesy of Cathy Winegar Davenport.)

When internal combustion engines were introduced to boats in the 1880s, the new gadgets left something to be desired in terms of horsepower and reliability. Sail and wind had been a part of Chesapeake Bay life for generations. Many people were skeptical that motors would take the place of sails. Early races between vessels often had sailboats winning, but as engines became more reliable, there was no question that motor-powered deck boats were here to stay. (Courtesy of Deltaville Maritime Museum.)

The schooner *Bohemia* in full sail was the main focus of this photograph taken at West Point, Virginia, in the 1930s. The transition from sail to power was taking place about that time, as a deck boat is shown moored at a wharf alongside a sailing schooner. By the 1950s, many of the bay's sailing schooners had been abandoned and left to rot along the shorelines of creeks and coves. Some had found new life and been converted to motor-powered deck boats. *Bohemia* was the last sailing schooner to carry lumber on the Bay. On January 2, 1950, *Bohemia* sank at a dock on the eastern branch of the Elizabeth River in Norfolk. She was raised and taken to Sarah Creek in Gloucester County, Virginia, where she later died. (Courtesy of the Dr. A.L. VanName Jr. collection.)

This November 1950 photograph taken at Sarah Creek shows *Bohemia* in her final days. She is moored alongside *Gladys L.* and *W.J. Matthews*, both former sailing schooners converted to power. *Gladys L.* was originally named *Miriam* and built by Joseph W. Brooks in Madison, Maryland, in 1903. *W.J. Matthews* was originally named *Dorchester* and built in 1882, also by Brooks. (Courtesy of the Dr. A.L. VanName Jr. collection.)

Norma was originally a sailing bugeye built by O. Lloyd of Salisbury, Maryland, in 1901. She was converted to power in 1922 and was engaged in running whiskey and Scottish malt (valued at $100,000) when her crew was caught by the US Coast Guard near Salisbury and taken to Baltimore, where the contraband was removed. This photograph was taken in 1951 on Urbanna Creek, when *Norma* was engaged in the legal freighting of grain. (Courtesy of the Dr. A.L. VanName Jr. collection.)

Mary Margaret was converted to a power vessel and offers an excellent example of how sailboats were disfigured in the conversion process. The vessel's bowsprit has been shortened, and a deck boat–style house/pilothouse has been installed. Maritime historians refer to these early converted-to-power sailboats as hybrids. (Courtesy of the Chesapeake Bay Maritime Museum.)

C.F. Miles, underway with its steadying sail up, was built by R.F. Miles of Oriole, Maryland, in 1909 as a sailing log hull bugeye. The 75-foot-long hull was built out of 13 logs. In the 1930s, around the time when this photograph was taken, she had recently been converted to power, as she still has her bowsprit leftover from her sailing days. *C.F. Miles* was part of a fleet of deck boats owned by J.H. Miles & Co. of Norfolk, Virginia. (Courtesy of John S. Rowan, Robert H. Burgess Collection, the Chesapeake Bay Maritime Museum collection.)

Masts on motorized deck boats were used to support a steadying sail, and a block and tackle was used to load and off-load freight and oysters. Masts were often roughly shaped in the forest by boatbuilders, hauled to a boatyard on a cart pulled by oxen, finished off at the yard, and installed on the boat. The masts were usually between 35 feet and 45 feet in height. This photograph was taken in King and Queen County, Virginia. This wood (for a mast) was cut out of the Dragon Run. (Courtesy of Jean Holman.)

Lula M. Phillips was a sailing schooner converted to a motor-powered deck boat. She was built in 1877 by William Benson of Oxford, Maryland, and originally named *Annie M. Leonard*. She kept her sails when she was rebuilt in 1913 in Bethal, Delaware, and renamed *Lula M. Phillips*. She was later converted to power, as shown in this photograph. (Courtesy of the William C. Hight collection.)

William Henry Ward of Deltaville owned *Lula M. Phillips* toward the end of the boat's life. Ward was born in Somerset County, Maryland, in 1896 and grew up in Crisfield, Maryland. He moved to Deltaville in 1924 after falling in love and marrying Virginia Harrow of Deltaville. Ward purchased the vessel in 1934 and was captain of her until he retired in 1972. He hauled freight and oysters with her and was a well-known, jovial figure around the bay. (Courtesy of the William C. Hight collection.)

This photograph shows *Sarah C. Conway* in 1950 after she had been converted to a motorized deck boat. Harvey Conway of Cambridge, Maryland, owned the vessel when she was powered by sail. The Conway family owned a fleet of sailing vessels named after family members. Many of Harvey's sailing craft were converted to power and used to haul freight on the bay. (Courtesy of the Dr. A.L. VanName Jr. collection.)

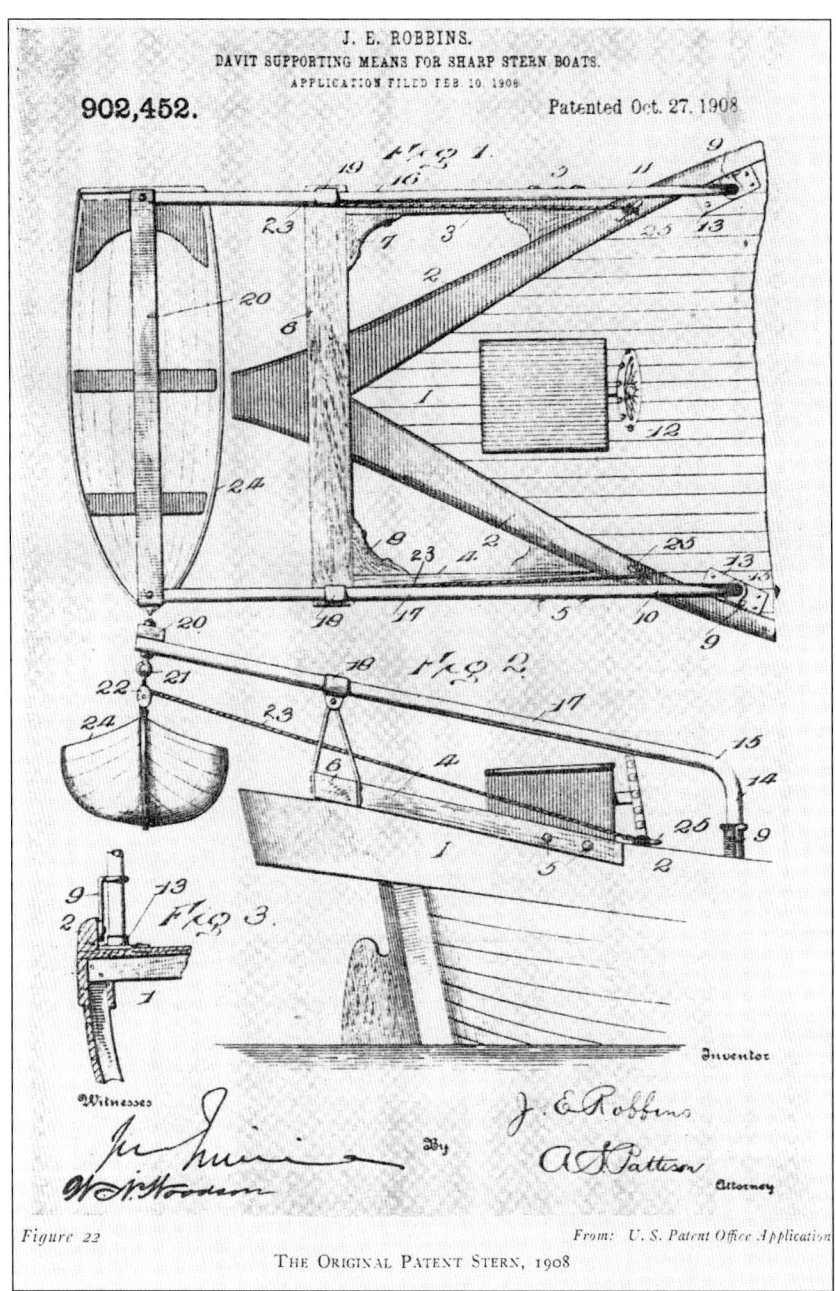

Figure 22 — The Original Patent Stern, 1908. From: U.S. Patent Office Application.

The patent stern, also called a drake stern, was a style of stern built onto sharp-ended bugeyes. Capt. Joseph E. Robbins of Cambridge, Maryland, developed and patented this style of stern in 1908. The style provided a means for supporting davits made of pipe and used to carry a push boat. Over time, the area between the V-deck and the pipes was filled in with planks or grating to provide more deck space. When converted to power, bugeyes did not require the use of a push boat. However, the patent stern style was kept because it provided added deck space. For every patent stern built on a vessel, Captain Robbins received a small royalty. On the bugeye *Gladys L.*, the extra space created by squaring off the outsides of the V was used to extend the house. *Gladys L.* was one of the biggest bugeyes and had a very large house. (Author's collection.)

John Branford was named for the builder who constructed the sail-powered bugeye in 1900 at Fairmount, Maryland. She was converted to power around 1937 and used as an oyster buyboat. She also hauled wheat, tomatoes, and watermelons. This photograph, taken in 1947, shows her patent stern. (Courtesy of the William C. Hight collection.)

For many years, *John Branford* was owned by Achilles T. Rowe of Locust Hill, Virginia. Rowe bought oysters in this boat on the Rappahannock River. Josh Holmes, born in 1914, said that he and his father Zachary sold oysters exclusively to Rowe. Some buyboat captains discriminated by paying less money to African Americans for a bushel. "Captain Rowe always paid us the same price for a bushel as he paid to whites," said Holmes. (Courtesy of the William C. Hight collection.)

John Branford was a two-mast bugeye before it was converted to power. The helmsman station on sailing vessels was located outside, near the stern, so the helmsman could see over and through the rigging. When this boat was converted to power, a tall house/pilothouse was built near the stern, allowing the helmsman to steer the boat from inside the pilothouse and out of the weather. (Courtesy of the Dr. A.L. VanName Jr. collection.)

Ida and Lula was built as a sailing bugeye in 1885 in Somerset County, Maryland. In this photograph, she has an outside steering rudder that remained from her days when she was a sailing vessel. Instead of a full cabin/pilothouse, the vessel has a pilothouse and engine room aft. Later, the pilothouse was extended aft to provide room for sleeping quarters and a galley. The vessel was owned by George L. Smith and Brothers of Sharps, Virginia. (Courtesy of James Smith.)

William Frederick "Fred" Ward of Urbanna, Virginia, was a late-19th/early-20th-century boatbuilder who built one of the first motorized deck boats in that area. Born in 1862, Ward built Crescent at George Chowning's railway in Urbanna in 1904. Ward could build any style of vessel. He rebuilt the 78-foot, two-masted sailing schooner Ida Mae in 1898. With the introduction of deadrise and cross-planked-bottom construction on the bay in the 1880s, early builders, like Ward, quickly picked up the relevant skills. The V-style bow built into deck boats allows the vessels to cut through choppy bay seas with relative ease. Ward was a pioneer in the transition from building sailboats to deadrise powerboats. (Courtesy of Wanda Greenwood Hollberg.)

Fred Ward built the Crescent in 1904. As a very early style of motorized deck boat, the Crescent was built with stem-to-stern bottom planking and a unique raised round stern. The arrival of the Crescent made the local newspaper, the Southside Sentinel, on December 15, 1905: "The gasoline boat Crescent, owned by Messrs. Clarkson, Garrett, and Hunt of Bowlers Wharf is on Chowning's Railway having her bottom coppered. Young Mr. Garrett is overseeing the job." (Courtesy of Wit Garrett.)

Ida Mae was originally named Jacob S. Barnes. After Fred Ward rebuilt her from the keel up in 1898, she was renamed, and Ward registered as her builder. Capt. Charlie Christopher of Deltaville, Virginia, was her longtime captain. She was owned by the Van Wagenen Bro. of Urbanna and used for hauling freight. She was never converted to power. (Courtesy of the Dr. A.L. VanName Jr. collection.)

Bosun chairs were used on sailboats and motor-powered deck boats to maintain mast and rigging. The chair was tied to a halyard line from a block and tackle on the mast. The bosun sat in the chair and was lifted up the mast by strong arms, rope, and block and tackle. This chair belonged to the deck boat *Muriel Eileen* and was used by her mate, the late Charlie Sayer of Urbanna, Virginia. (Courtesy of Nancy Sayer Lewis.)

This photograph shows the back of the bosun chair and how rope is tied together and threaded through the wooden seat. When rigging tangled or broke at the top of the mast, the bosun was lifted up to untangle the problem. The chair was seldom used but was a necessary tool on the boat. (Courtesy of Nancy Sayer Lewis.)

This classic water barrel—used for storing drinking water—was on the stern of the *Iva W.* in 1984. This same style of barrel had been used for generations on Chesapeake Bay sailing craft. Capt. Johnny Ward, who had *Iva W.* built in 1929, got this barrel and holding stand off a sailing schooner. The cabinet shown here held glasses and cups. (Author's collection.)

During the early years of motor-powered deck boats, steadying sails were used to keep the boats on course in choppy seas and to provide power. Sails were part of the evolution of modern-day deck boats, as early boats lacked the motor power needed to maneuver the bay's seas without the additional support of a sail. (Courtesy of the Dr. A.L. VanName Jr. collection.)

Two

Log Boats

The Chesapeake Bay log canoe was one of the first platforms used by commercial fishermen on the bay to harvest fish, crabs, and oysters. When the first English settlers arrived in 1607, they saw Native Americans using single log dugout canoes. Realizing the seaworthiness of the log canoe, English boatbuilders began to piece logs together to enlarge hulls. Logs were pegged together with locust trunnels and, later, iron pins. Sailing canoes made from three and five logs were abundant in Maryland and Virginia waters.

Although most deck boats were made from planks, 20th-century log canoe builders carried on the traditions of the 18th- and 19th-century craft by building motor-powered boats out of logs. These boats worked well in the oyster and crab-dredge fisheries, as the sides were lower to the water than those of standard plank-built deck boats. Only two motor-powered deck boats built specifically for power have survived until today. The 1924 *F.D. Crockett* has been meticulously restored by the Deltaville Maritime Museum, and the 1909 *Old Point* was restored by the Chesapeake Bay Maritime Museum.

One of the most beautiful and oldest deck boats on Chesapeake Bay is *William B. Tennison*, which is owned by the Calvert Marine Museum in Solomons, Maryland. The vessel was built in 1899 as a nine-log sailing bugeye by Frank Laird of Monie, Maryland. She was converted to an oyster buyboat in 1906–1907. The boat was listed in the National Register of Historic Places in 1980 and became a National Historic Landmark in 1994. (Courtesy of Hannah Straub.)

The nine-log hull of the bugeye *Edna E. Lockwood* shows how logs were positioned in sail and motorized log boats. *Edna E. Lockwood* was constructed in 1889 by boatbuilder John B. Harrison at Tilghman Island, Maryland. The vessel was never converted to power. However, *Old Point*, shown in the background, is a seven-log hull motorized deck boat built in 1909 by J.G. Wornom of Poquoson, Virginia. (Courtesy of the Chesapeake Bay Maritime Museum.)

This photograph shows the monkey rail and stern on *Old Point*. *Old Point* was built in Poquoson, Virginia, a center of log-canoe building. Many log deck boats were handcrafted by Poquoson builders. The boat is owned—and well maintained—by the Chesapeake Bay Maritime Museum in St. Michaels, Maryland. She was built as a powerboat. (Author's collection.)

Although this is not a Chesapeake Bay log deck boat, it provides an example of an attempt to convert a log sailboat to a motor-powered vessel. The engine is positioned as close to the stern as possible, and a small house is built around it to protect it from the elements. This style eventually led to the development of Chesapeake Bay deck boats. (Courtesy of the Deltaville Maritime Museum.)

In this September 2005 image, the log boat *F.D. Crockett* is being towed from Poquoson into Jackson Creek in Deltaville, Virginia, by the deck boat *East Hampton*. *F.D. Crockett* was a gift to the Deltaville Maritime Museum, and this moment was the start of a lengthy rebuild that resulted in the complete restoration of the log canoe built in 1924 for Ferdinand Desota Crockett of Seaford, Virginia. (Author's collection.)

Weathered and worn, *F.D. Crockett* was still seaworthy enough to make the trip from Poquoson to Deltaville in 2005. Skeptics questioned whether the vessel could be restored, but through the efforts of boatwright John England and the crew of the Deltaville Maritime Museum, the boat is alive and well today. (Author's collection.)

The log boat *F.D. Crockett* has a beautiful fan-tail stern. The stern has a rounded spoon shape; this style evolved from the V-shape built into the bows and sterns of log canoes. As customers requested more rounded sterns, variations of round sterns on bay deck boats were built into the vessels. (Courtesy of John England.)

This is an early photograph of Smith Marine Railway in Dare, Virginia, with a deck boat up on the rails. The Smith family established the railway on Chisman's Creek in 1842. John and Kirby Smith built two log deck boats at the railway. The log boat *Isle of York* was built there in 1925, and *Ethel L.*, a round-stern log deck boat, was built in 1927. (Courtesy of Smith Marine Railway.)

This log boat is on the railway at Reedville Marine Railway in Reedville, Virginia. Through the 1920s, 1930s, and 1940s, boatwrights had to be proficient in repairing log boats as well as planked-built deck boats. Reedville Marine Railway was founded in the 1890s and, over the years, saw the evolution from sail to motor-powered boats. (Courtesy of George and Becky Butler.)

George P. Butler (standing in the foreground) of Reedville Marine Railway is repairing a skipjack used in Maryland's public oyster-dredge fishery. Butler's good reputation for being able to repair all kinds of wooden boats kept him and his yard busy. Today, the yard is run by George P.'s son George M. Butler. (Courtesy of George and Becky Butler.)

Gilbert White of Lancaster County, Virginia, started his career in boatbuilding as a log canoe builder. The stern on *Elva C.* was built by White in 1922 with large chunks of wood used to shape the rounded elliptical stern. This was a technique White learned as a builder of log canoes, often using chunks of wood to shape the V in the bow and stern on log canoes. During the transition from logs to planks, some aspects of log-boat construction found their way into the more modern deadrise and cross-planked wooden boats. This chunk stern is a throwback to log canoe building. *Elva C.* is built out of planks and is now owned by the Reedville Fishermen's Museum in Reedville. (Author's collection.)

George M. Butler has worked on deck boats for much of his life. He is one of just a few craftsmen on the Chesapeake who can still make a chunk stern like the one he shaped when repairing *Elva C*. The Butler family has owned Reedville Marine Railway since 1906. The extended life of wooden log and planked-built deck boats is closely tied to knowledgeable craftsmen who, over time, have continued to maintain the boats. (Author's collection.)

This photograph reveals the inside of a chunk stern on the deck boat *Peggy*, showing how chunks of wood are fitted together to shape a round stern, also called a logged stern. This construction style evolved from the methods used by early log canoe builders. Chunks or blocks of wood were shaped to form the stern and laid in layers one on top of another. The butt joints are staggered so that joints do not overlap and create a seam where water can penetrate. (Author's collection.)

A view of the outside of the same round chunk stern shows a dressed or smoothed-down logged stern. The term "dressing the stern" is used by boatbuilders to refer to shaping and smoothing down the chunks. The smooth edges of chunks are shaped with a foot or lip adz and other tools. When the stern is painted, chunk seams cannot be seen, so this method creates a pretty, round-shaped stern. (Author's collection.)

William Rollins of Poquoson, Virginia, is shown using a lip adz to chop out the hull of the five-log canoe he was building in 1988. Rollins built the last log canoe in Poquoson and was the last commercial log-canoe boatbuilder in Virginia. He named this boat *Holly June*, and it is still owned by the Rollins family. (Author's collection.)

A lip adz, axe, and log-puller are on display in this photograph taken inside the William Rollins boat shop in Poquoson. Rollins learned to build log canoes during his summers working at Bennett's Railway in Poquoson as a teenager and later at J.S. Darling's railway in Hampton. He learned the trade from renowned builder Clyde Smith and others while working at the railways. (Author's collection.)

F.D. Crockett, Old Point, and William B. Tennison are the last log hull deck boats in existence on the bay. The boats are floating museums and are maintained, respectively, by the Deltaville Maritime Museum in Deltaville, Virginia; Chesapeake Bay Maritime Museum in St. Michaels, Maryland; and Calvert Marine Museum in Solomons, Maryland. (Courtesy of Michaela Chowning.)

Three

Freight and Passenger boats

Freight boats—sometimes called bay freighters and/or packet boats—were used on the bay to haul passengers and freight. The bay's freight business was a throwback to the days of sailing schooners and bugeyes. Sailing vessels were used to haul bulk commodities such as lumber, coal, fertilizer, cordwood, hogs, corn, wheat, soybeans, watermelons, and other farm produce. Following the transition from sails to motors, deck boats took over the freight trade. The boats were used by steamboat companies and others to haul freight from isolated docks that did not have enough freight or passenger business to warrant using a large steamboat.

Small-town merchants owned deck boats that they used to travel to Baltimore; Washington, DC; and Norfolk. There, they purchased city goods and brought back the merchandise to sell to their local customers. Baltimore-based vegetable-canning firms owned large deck boats that were used to haul cans, sugar, and other goods from Baltimore to canning houses scattered throughout the bay region. When processing was complete, boats hauled the finished canned product back to Baltimore for sale.

The largest deck boat built on the bay, the 100-foot *Marydel*, was owned by W.E. Valliant & Co. of Delaware and used to haul fertilizer. From June until around the first of September, boatloads of watermelons were hauled from North Carolina, Maryland, and Virginia to markets in Baltimore and Washington, DC.

Deck boat captains traveled by way of the Intracoastal Waterway to reach North Carolina growers near Elizabeth City, Edenton, and Coinjock. The boats hauled freight and passengers from Crisfield, Maryland, and Cape Charles and Reedville, Virginia, to the isolated islands of Smith and Tangier, transporting groceries, gasoline, lumber, small automobiles, and people to and from the islands.

The State of Maryland's only official school boat—a deck boat—transported schoolchildren from Smith Island to Crisfield High School. Corn, soybeans, and wheat grown by Tidewater farmers were hauled by boat to Norfolk and Salisbury, Maryland.

As the quality of roads and trucks improved, the freighting business shifted away from deck boats to overland trucking.

Just as businesses now own trucks to haul products to and from their stores, merchant owners in the early 20th century owned deck boats and hauled merchandise from wholesale houses in Norfolk and Baltimore back to their stores. *Secret* was owned by Sam Richardson of S.E. Richardson's Pharmacy in Urbanna, Virginia. Richardson also hired out the boat to other merchants in town. (Courtesy of Sam Richardson.)

Throughout the bay region, small businesses like S.E. Richardson's Pharmacy in Urbanna invested in deck boats. Richardson used the boat to support his business, but in the summertime, his family and friends enjoyed Sunday afternoon cruises and fishing trips on *Secret*. (Courtesy of Pat Marshall.)

The era of motorized deck boats overlapped the days of steamboats and sailing schooners. This photograph shows them all together. The deck boat is close to shore and loaded with watermelons soon to be bound for markets in Baltimore or Washington, DC. The steamboat coming in on the left is arriving at Conrad's Wharf on the Piankatank River, while a two-mast sailing schooner at right is waiting to be loaded with either watermelons or lumber. (Courtesy of Nola Watson.)

From late June to September, sweet, red, and ripe Congo and Georgia Rattlesnake watermelons were hauled from the melon fields in Virginia, Maryland, and North Carolina. Farmers brought the melons to wharves via horse and wagon to load them onto motorized deck boats. The melons were hauled to Baltimore's Long Dock before being sold at the market. The pickers shown here are awaiting the arrival of a deck boat to load the watermelons. (Courtesy of Nola Watson.)

During watermelon season, many deck boat captains and crews would go as far as Elizabeth City, Edenton, and Coinjock, North Carolina, to buy loads of melons from growers. At docks in Baltimore and Washington, DC, watermelons were sold retail off the boat or wholesale to chain grocery stores. Crew members sold melons directly off the boat to customers driving by with their car windows down—this was referred to as "legging watermelons." (Author's collection.)

Thelma W. is named for Thelma Wake, the wife of the boat's captain and owner, Willard H. Wake of Amburg, Virginia. This photograph shows the deck boat moored in Core's Creek (sometimes called Providence Creek) on the Piankatank River in front of the Wakes' home. Captain Wake freighted watermelons and barrels from Baltimore and bought oysters. (Courtesy of John Wake.)

This stern photograph of *Andrew J. Lewis* provides an aft view of a double deckhouse on a deck boat. Double deckhouses were usually built into larger vessels (70 feet and larger). Larger boats were mainly used to haul freight and grain. Some large boats hauled freight between the Caribbean and Chesapeake and were at sea for extended periods. (Courtesy of Edwin W. Rice.)

Conrad's Wharf on Piankatank River was regularly frequented by deck boats picking up and offloading freight. A barrel factory was located on the premises. Barrels were made there and used to transport cucumbers, potatoes, and whiskey. When awaiting shipment on a deck boat, barrels loaded with potatoes and cucumbers were lined up along the wharf. When barrels were loaded with whiskey, they were locked in a storage shed. A barrel hook—used to load the barrels—is visible on the far right in this photograph. (Courtesy of Nola Watson.)

Lillian T., later named *Pearl Faye*, was owned by Capt. Robert Dea Ailsworth of Deltaville, Virginia, and worked in the bay's watermelon, cantaloupe, and Irish potato trades. Potatoes were hauled to Baltimore and Washington, DC, in 13-peck barrels, while watermelons and cantaloupes were piled in the hold and on deck. Later, Todd Parks owned the *Pearl Faye* and used her to buy and haul soft-shell crabs from Tangier Island to Crisfield, Maryland. (Courtesy of Joe Conboy.)

Louise J. was built by Linwood Price of Deltaville, Virginia, in 1926. When this photograph was taken, the boat was owned by Thomas "Captain Tom" Yates Johnston of Amburg, Virginia. The boat is shown loaded with lumber at Conrad's Wharf on the Piankatank River. (Courtesy of Nola Watson.)

The 80-foot *G.T. Forbush* was built in 1951 by Charles Henry Rice of Reedville, Virginia. This photograph shows the vessel nearly complete with top portions of the double deckhouse/pilothouse under construction. During his boatbuilding career, Rice constructed many boats—but only three deck boats. He built *Verna R.* for himself in 1947, naming it after his wife, and *Rebecca Forbush* in 1947 for Gus Forbush, who used the vessel to haul freight. (Courtesy of Edwin W. Rice.)

The 80-foot *Colony* was used to haul corn and wheat from grain facilities on the western shore of the Chesapeake Bay to Norfolk, Virginia. She was built in 1930 by Linwood Price as a 60-foot deck boat. In the 1950s, Lee Deagle at Deagle & Son Marine Railway in Deltaville cut her in two and added 20 feet to her hull for owner Howard Ward of Crisfield, Maryland. (Courtesy of Joe Conboy.)

This photograph, taken in 1948 at Gwynn's Island in Mathews County, Virginia, shows an unidentified deck boat. The boat was most likely used to haul freight, as she is rigged with double-hatch doors for loading the hold and has a large house and forepeak for accommodating crew. (Courtesy of the Dr. A.L. VanName collection.)

Elsie Louise was owned by Morattico Packing Co. of Baltimore, Maryland, and used to haul freight and canning products. The boat was built in 1914 by J. Wood Tull in Irvington, Virginia. Today, the hull of *Elsie Louise* is alive and known as *Veteran*; she is being used as a tour boat in Urbanna, Virginia. (Courtesy of Selden Richardson.)

Deck boats were often named after family members. Muriel and Eileen Roberts are pictured here on a couple of mules next to their father, R.E. Roberts, owner of Lord-Mott Company in Baltimore. In 1926, when R.E. Roberts had J.W. Smith of Bena, Virginia, build him a 60-foot deck boat, he named it *Muriel Eileen* after his two daughters. Two years later, he had Smith build him a larger boat and also named it *Muriel Eileen*. Thereafter, the boats were known as Big *Muriel Eileen* and Little *Muriel Eileen*. (Courtesy of David Cantera.)

The double-decker Big *Muriel Eileen* served R.E. Roberts and Lord-Mott Company into the 1960s. The 80-foot-vessel sank in 1969 in the Atlantic Ocean while working in a clam-dredging fishery. The vessel between the Big *Muriel Eileen* and the bulkhead is the converted-to-power bugeye *John Branford*. (Courtesy of the William C. Hight collection.)

This photograph of *Marydel* shows the expanse of deck space on what was the largest deck boat ever built on the bay. *Marydel*—the name is a combination of "Maryland" and "Delaware"—was exclusively used for freight, primarily to haul fertilizer for W.E. Valliant & Co. in Delaware. It was built in 1927 by Linwood Price at his boatyard on Fishing Bay. (Author's collection.)

Russell Parker of Wake, Virginia, built several deck boats for his own use. *Frances* is not a deck boat but was used by Parker to carry passengers and mail. Parker had a contract with a steamboat company to transport passengers and mail to Mill Creek Steamboat Dock from the steamer when weather or the tide did not allow the vessel to enter the creek. When the weather was too bad for *Frances*, Parker used the deck boat *Juanita*, which is shown here moored next to *Frances*. (Author's collection.)

In this photograph, *Nellie Jane* is bound for Tangier Island with a small car aboard. Roads on Tangier and Smith Islands are narrow and can only be maneuvered using golf carts or small cars. Since there are no bridges to the islands, which are both located in the middle of Chesapeake Bay, deck boats are used to haul unusual freight to and from them. (Courtesy of Lewis Parks.)

Four

Buying and Planting Seed Oysters

By the early 1800s, oystermen from Staten Island had depleted their natural oyster beds by overharvesting them and began taking small oysters and planting them on local beds, thereby growing oysters. After seeing the success of New England oystermen, Chesapeake Bay oyster farmers began planting and growing oysters in a similar manner. Prior to the introduction of motor-powered boats, sailing schooners and sloops were used to buy seed oysters from James River hand-tongers. Once the vessels were loaded with seed, they sailed to rivers, creeks, and coves to broadcast the seed—using hands and shovels—onto private oyster beds. Today, deck boat crews use high-pressure water hoses to blow seed off the deck and onto oyster beds.

The business of growing oysters escalated in Virginia in the 1890s partly due to the state establishing legal private oyster beds. The Virginia legislature authorized Lt. James Bowen Baylor of the US Coast and Geodetic Survey to survey 143,000 acres of oyster grounds for public use and 110,000 acres to be set aside for private growers. Private beds were owned by the state but could be leased by growers for an annual fee. By 1894, Baylor had completed his survey and established boundaries for public and private oyster grounds in Virginia waters. This single act encouraged and inspired private enterprise to grow and expand the oyster business and has played a major role in the modern success of Virginia's oyster-farming businesses.

With increased growth, demand also grew for motorized deck boats to work in the oyster fishery. The number of deck boats being built peaked in the 1920s. The oyster diseases MSX and dermo crippled the bay's oyster fishery from the 1960s through the 1990s. However, with recent developments in disease-resistant oysters, the states of Virginia and Maryland have seen a revival in oyster farming.

Today, deck boats are used in Virginia's private oyster-farming business and in the State of Maryland's Oyster Replenishment Program to replenish the state's public oyster grounds. With this, several old deck boats have found new life and are being rebuilt to carry on the centuries-old tradition of buying and planting seed oysters.

When this photograph was taken in 1970 of Little *Muriel Eileen* loaded down with seed oysters, the boat was owned by the Ward family of Deltaville, Virginia. Capt. Johnny Ward and his three sons—Floyd, Melvin, and Milton—owned numerous deck boats and bought seed oysters from James River oystermen and planted seed on private grounds throughout Virginia waters. (Courtesy of the *Gloucester-Mathews Gazette-Journal*.)

The 65-foot *Nellie Crockett* was built by Charles A. Dana of Crisfield, Maryland, in 1925. In this 1984 picture, she is loaded down with 1,852 bushels of seed oysters bound for private beds near Water View on the Rappahannock River. The seed was purchased from hand-tong oystermen on James River by then-owner and captain of *Nellie*, James Ward. (Author's collection.)

The 60-foot-long *J.C. Drewer* was built in 1929 by Linwood Price of Deltaville, Virginia. The vessel was owned for many years by Capt. Robert Dea Ailsworth of Deltaville. Captain Dea used the boat to buy and plant seed oysters and to haul watermelons and freight to Baltimore and Norfolk. When this photograph was taken, she was being used in Maryland waters to plant shell and seed. (Courtesy of the Chesapeake Bay Maritime Museum; photograph by Richard Dodds.)

Capt. Robert Dea Ailsworth and his wife, Lelia Bratten Ailsworth, are pictured here in 1916. They had 11 children, and Captain Dea made his living working deck boats. He owned *J.C. Drewer* and *Lillian T.* and used the boats to buy and plant oysters and to haul freight. (Courtesy of Alfred E. Ailsworth Jr.)

These seed oysters on *Nellie Crockett* were purchased on James River and planted on Rappahannock River. When boats arrived late in the day or during bad weather, they laid over in creeks near the planting grounds. This photograph was taken on Urbanna Creek after the boat had laid over for a night. (Author's collection.)

When planting seed oysters, a mate uses the edge of a shovel to lower the pile along the sides. When the pile is lowered enough, seed can be shoveled from the deck, as shown here. Using a shovel is a traditional method of planting seed. In more recent years, seed and shell are blown off the deck with high-pressure water hoses. (Author's collection.)

The idea of planting seed oysters on Chesapeake Bay was introduced to the region in the mid-1700s by New York, New Jersey, and Connecticut oystermen. The deck boat Mobjack is shown loaded down with oysters at Gwynn's Island, Virginia, in 1998. The 72-foot Mobjack and her sister ship Ocean View were built for J.H. Miles & Co., based in Norfolk, Virginia, sometime after World War II. After the war, J.H. Miles & Co. predicted a resurgence in demand for oysters and had Linwood Price in Deltaville build the two boats to meet that anticipated demand. Mobjack, with its 25-foot beam, has a wide enough deck for a small motorized Bobcat to maneuver and be used to load and off-load oysters. The boat was designed with a five-foot, five-inch draft to allow her to work on J.H. Miles & Co.'s shallow oyster beds on Mobjack Bay and the York and James Rivers. Ocean View is still alive but in bad shape. (Author's collection.)

Iva W. and *Lula M. Phillips* are pictured here loaded with James River seed oysters on their way to being planted on Rappahannock River. When vessels are underway, automobile tires are used to keep oysters from sliding into the water. The larger *Lula M. Phillips* was originally built as a sail-powered schooner and converted to power; as the photograph shows, she held considerably more payload than *Iva W.* (Courtesy of the William C. Hight collection.)

Automobile tires dangle over the side of the deck boat *Inez* as the crew off-loads seed oysters onto oyster grounds. *Inez* was constructed by boatbuilder Buddy Sable in 1936 for Capt. Russell Parker of Wake, Virginia. Sable was paid 40¢ per hour to build the boat, and his three helpers received 25¢ per hour. (Courtesy of the William C. Hight collection.)

This closer view of *Inez* shows the crew shoveling seed and the captain directing the operation in the pilothouse. The stain on the pilothouse walls shows how high oysters were stacked against the house. Shoveling 1,800 bushels of oysters off the deck was no easy task for two men. (Courtesy of the William C. Hight collection.)

Inez was built—using no plans—in Russell Parker's backyard on Mill Creek on Rappahannock River. The lines of *Inez* were laid out by Parker with a pencil on a wide pine board. All lumber was cut locally and taken to Bridger's Planing Mill in Deltaville, where the lumber was dressed. (Courtesy of the William C. Hight collection.)

Estelle Leonard was built in 1927 by Jabez Tyler in Cambridge, Maryland. She was owned by Wayne W. Evans of Crisfield. She has flip doors along her decks for off-loading seed oysters onto oyster grounds. Alongside *Estelle Leonard* is a Smith Island crab scrape boat (called a barcat on Tangier Island) used to catch peeler and soft-shell crabs. (Courtesy of the Chesapeake Bay Maritime Museum; photograph by Richard Dodds.)

Francis Randolph Goddard of Piney Point, Maryland, built the deck boat *Poppa Francis* in 1989 to be used to haul seed oysters for the State of Maryland. "I never built a leaking boat, and I've built 160 some boats," he said in an interview in 2010. Goddard is one of the last living people to have built a deck boat on Chesapeake Bay. (Author's collection.)

Boatbuilder Francis Goddard is a legend in southern Maryland boatbuilding corners, and here, he is pictured with his cat, Tom Cat. Goddard built the sailing skipjack *Connie Francis* in 1984 and the 65-foot deck boat *Poppa Francis* in 1989. When Goddard was 10 years old, he asked his father to buy him a skiff. When his father said, "Go build it yourself," that is what Francis did. He pulled lumber off the side of his father's tobacco barn and built a 16-foot skiff. During his lifetime, Goddard built over 160 wooden boats varying in size from a 12-foot skiff to a 65-foot deadrise boat. He built *Poppa Francis* for his own use and worked the boat for many years in the State of Maryland's Oyster Replenishment Program. *Poppa Francis* and Goddard have regularly attended the annual Chesapeake Bay Buyboat Rendezvous. (Author's collection.)

With the revival of Virginia's oyster fishery, some deck boats have been restored for dredging oysters and planting seed. Oysterman Richard Green of Hayes, Virginia, restored Mobjack in 2019 and is using her to work 2,000 acres of oyster grounds that he leases from the state. Mobjack was built in 1946 by Linwood Price for J.H. Miles & Co. of Norfolk, Virginia. (Author's collection.)

The door system used for planting oysters (as shown in the photograph of Estelle Leonard on page 54) is a relatively modern method of dispersing seed oysters from deck boats. An even more modern method is the use of PVC pipe. The pipe is fitted into holes, as shown on the side of the deck boat Mobjack. When oystermen are ready to plant shell or seed oysters, the PVC pipes are pulled out, and oysters spill over into the water. (Author's collection.)

Another new innovation in planting seed oysters is the use of high-pressure water hoses to blow shell and seed oysters off the deck and into the water. As part of the restoration of *Mobjack*, Richard Green installed this high-pressure hose for use in maintaining his oyster beds on the James and York Rivers. (Author's collection).

Historically, the shovel has been the main tool used to plant seed oysters. On October 9, 1985, Capt. James Ward bought 1,852 bushels of James River seed oysters from oystermen on Deep Creek in Newport News, Virginia. The load was planted in the traditional manner, as shown here, on grounds leased by Donald Morton of Water View near Punchbowl Point on Rappahannock River. (Author's collection.)

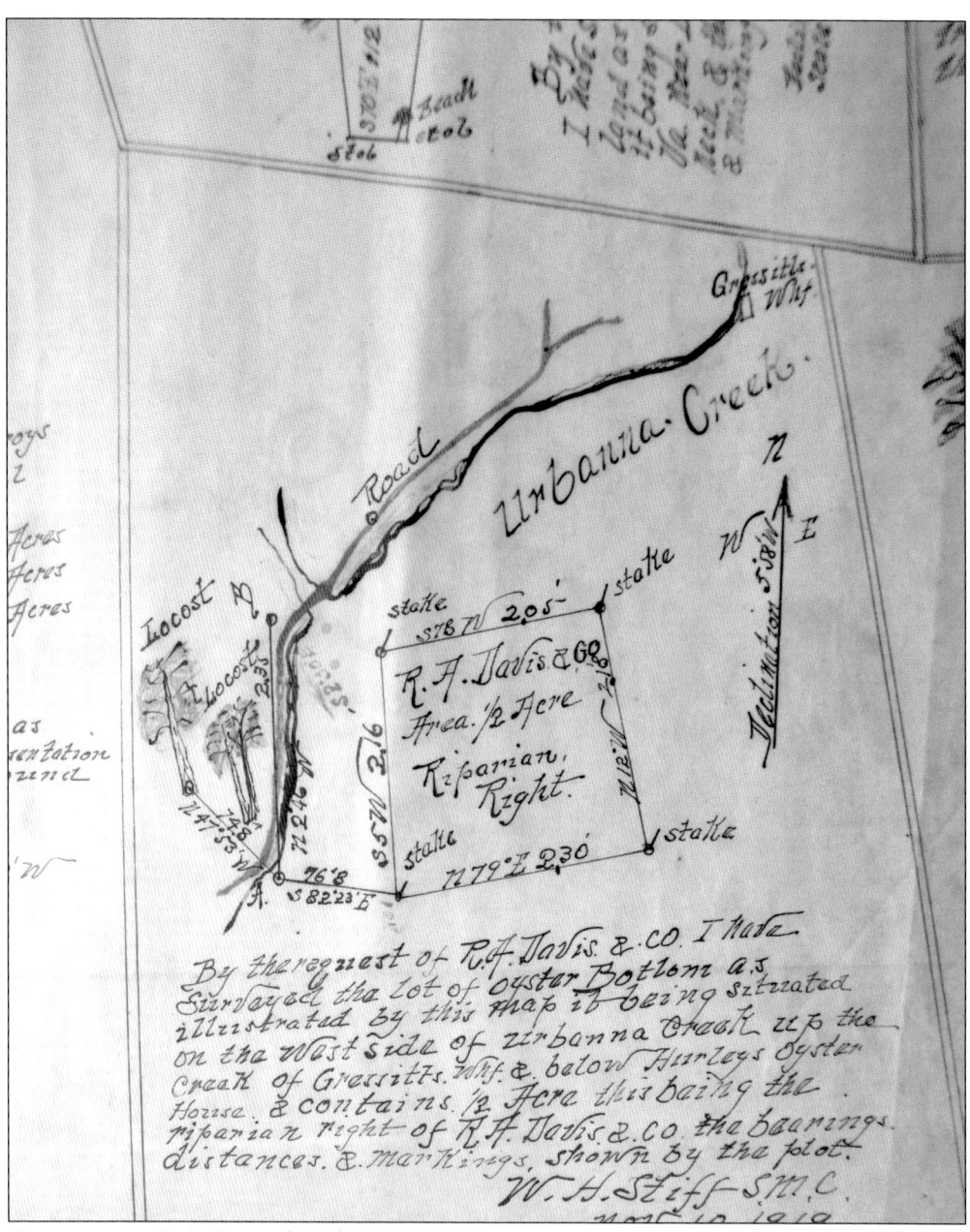

Oyster grower R.A. Davis, based in Urbanna, maintained this half-acre of oyster bottom for oyster storage. Market changes sometimes left retail oyster prices below profit margins. While waiting for prices to rise, Davis used his half-acre bottom for storage of market-size oysters. He leased large acreage of oyster bottom in the Rappahannock River for planting and growing. When necessary, market-size oysters from riverbeds were off-loaded onto the half-acre. Davis's creek bed was also utilized when there was an extended freeze and boats were unable to come and go to his river oyster beds. Davis could access oysters from the creek bed by making a hole in the ice and having oystermen stand on the ice and tong up oysters with hand tongs. This way, he could meet customer demand while many of his competitors had to wait for the weather to break. (Courtesy of Middlesex County Clerk's Office.)

Five

OYSTER AND CRAB DREDGING

The introduction of new types of fishing gear has often produced some exciting times, but none provided more lore and color than the dredge. The dredge was introduced on the bay around the start of the 19th century, when New England oystermen came south looking to harvest oysters on the Chesapeake.

The gear was so efficient that in 1811, the Virginia General Assembly passed a law prohibiting the use of the dredge. Maryland lawmakers followed Virginia's course in 1820 and passed a similar law. Later, Virginia approved a law allowing the use of the dredge on vessels working on private oyster grounds. Maryland lawmakers passed a law restricting the use of the dredge to only sail-powered vessels. This resulted in Maryland's oyster skipjack fleet. Today, the fleet is the last commercial sailing fleet in North America. Virginia's law allowing the dredge to be used on private oyster grounds and when harvesting crabs in the winter resulted in the building of a large Virginia fleet of deck boats.

About the same time motor-powered deck boats came on the Chesapeake scene, Virginia began issuing licenses for the harvesting of blue crabs. The licensing began in 1904, but the exact year watermen started dredging crabs is unknown. Surely, it was before the beginning of the 20th century, and legend has it that watermen working oyster dredges out of Hampton Roads ventured a little too far over into the bay's channel and brought up a lick full of sooks (female hard crabs). This eventually led to Virginia's winter crab-dredge fishery, where about 80 percent of the harvest was female crabs.

The large winter harvest of the female crabs led the Virginia Marine Resources Commission to close the winter crab-dredge fishery season starting in 2008. However, the fishery extended the working life of bay deck boats and is a primary reason why so many Chesapeake Bay deck boats are still around today.

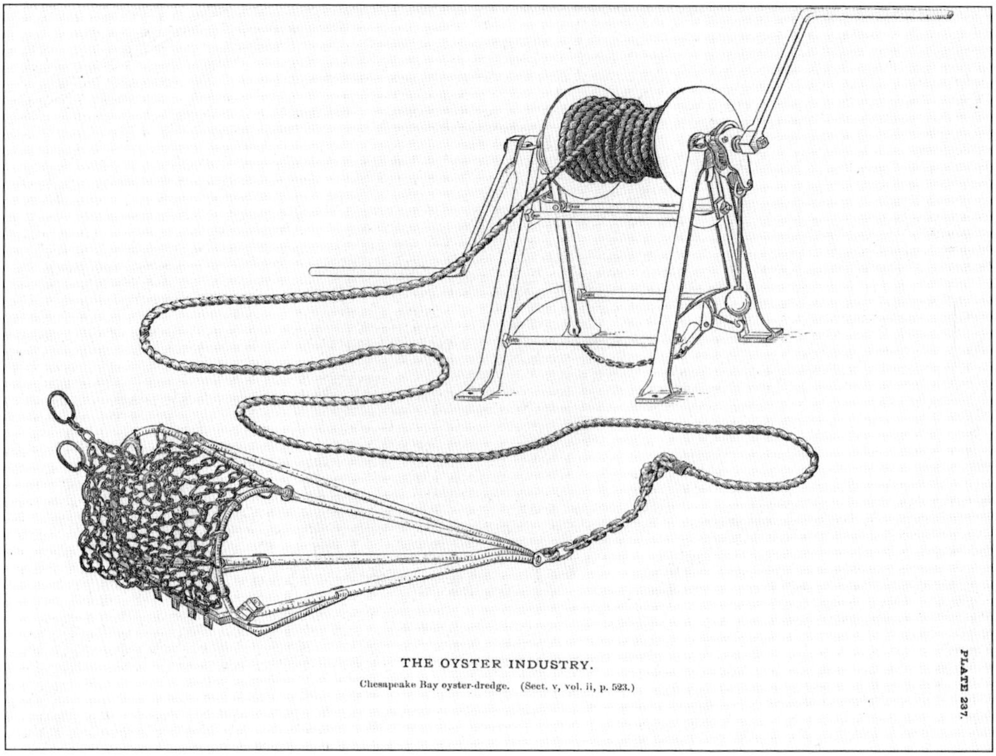

THE OYSTER INDUSTRY.
Chesapeake Bay oyster-dredge. (Sect. v, vol. ii, p. 523.)

At the start of the 19th century, the dredge and hand-winder were introduced to the Chesapeake Bay region by northern oystermen. The dredge was much more efficient than hand tongs, and because of this, it eventually led to out-and-out battles between oystermen working hand tongs and dredgers. The introduction of the dredge sparked the legendary oyster wars of the Chesapeake that lasted for over 150 years. (Courtesy of the Virginia Institute of Marine Science.)

This hand-operated oyster- and crab-dredge winder was used on the Potomac River to haul a dredge. This style of device was used on sail-powered schooners, bugeyes, skipjacks, and motor-powered deck boats. Over time, the strong arms of men turning the handle were replaced with mechanical tools—a much less burdensome way to haul up the dredge. (Author's collection.)

Dredge boats are rigged with a dredge post that supports two chains, two pulleys, and two dredges. A chain goes from the dredge through the pulleys down below deck to a winder that is powered off the main engine. After a day of dredging, the crew of *Iva W.* on Jackson Creek are shown fastening the dredges for the night. A safety rope extending down from the mast is being hooked to the dredge to keep it secure while on deck. (Courtesy of Carlos Smith.)

Ward Bros., originally named *Andrew J. Lewis* and built at E.C. Rice & Son boatyard at Fairport, Virginia, is shown dredging crabs in the winter of 1985. *Ward Bros.* was renamed for the sons of Capt. Johnny Ward of Deltaville, all of whom owned and worked deck boats. The brothers are Captains Floyd, the late Milton (or "Mitt"), and Melvin Ward. (Author's collection.)

This photograph of *Olive Virginia* working in Virginia's winter crab-dredge fishery was taken by Carlos Smith from the deck boat *Iva W.* in 1977. There are four other deck boats in the background dredging for crabs. *Olive Virginia* was built in 1926 by brothers John and T.W. "Tom" Wright of Deltaville, Virginia. (Courtesy of Carlos Smith.)

The deck boat *Mobjack* was built 25 feet wide and needed all that space to handle automatic oyster-dredge gear designed to dredge up oysters, drop the bivalves from the dredge onto a conveyor, and automatically off-load them into the hold. When this photograph was taken in 1964, *Mobjack* belonged to J.H. Miles & Co., which was based in Norfolk. (Courtesy of Joe Conboy.)

The 72-foot *Ocean View* was built for J.H. Miles & Co. of Norfolk in 1949. She was one of two of the company's oyster deck boats designed in 1945 by C.T. Forsberg of Freeport, Long Island, New York. After a rough life in the New Jersey oyster-dredge fishery, *Ocean View* is barely alive and is owned by oysterman Richard Green of Gloucester County, Virginia. (Courtesy of Joe Conboy.)

Nora W., originally named *Amanda C.*, was built for C.F.C. Haislip of Harryhogan, Virginia, in 1941. She was later owned by Johnny Ward and renamed for his mother, Nora Ward of Crisfield. *Nora W.* (at right in the below image) ended up on Tilghman Island, Maryland, and was renamed *Crow Brothers*. She laid derelict at the dock for many years before being taken out of the water and cut up. In this photograph, she is being used in Virginia's crab-dredge fishery. (Courtesy of Carlos Smith.)

Thomas W. was originally named *P.E. Pruitt* after its owner, Paul Pruitt, who was from Tangier Island. She was built in Crisfield, Maryland, in 1935 by Howard & Smith. When this photograph was taken, the vessel was being worked in the Virginia crab-dredge fishery. Today, the boat has been meticulously converted into a yacht by owner Kevin Flynn of Philadelphia, Pennsylvania, who reestablished its original name, *P.E. Pruitt*. (Author's collection.)

The crab-dredge fishery provided good winter jobs for Chesapeake Bay watermen. The fishery was extremely dangerous, however, as watermen often had to work on slippery, icy decks in extremely cold weather. A slip overboard or a slip on the deck and a desperate grab for a dredge chain while in gear could mean a loss of life or the loss of fingers and/or hands. (Author's collection.)

This photograph was taken in December 1985 in Chesapeake Bay aboard the deck boat *Iva W.* The two-man crew is shown emptying the dredge bag full of crabs onto the deck. Circular handholders attached to the bottom of the dredge bag allow crewmen to flip the crabs out of the bag and onto the deck. (Author's collection.)

Blue crabs caught in Virginia's winter crab-dredge fishery were sold by the barrel to Virginia and Maryland crab-picking houses. Eighty percent of the crabs caught in the winter fishery were female. Conservation pressure eventually led to strict restrictions on catches, and the winter fishery season was closed by the Virginia Marine Resources Commission in 2008. (Author's collection.)

Here, barrels of female blue crabs are being off-loaded from the deck of *Iva W.* onto the deck of *Thomas W.* after a day of dredging near the cut channel in Chesapeake Bay. The unidentified mate at left is passing a barrel to Capt. Floyd Ward. On that day, the crew of *Iva W.* caught eight barrels of sooks and six baskets of jimmies, considered a poor day of crabbing. (Author's collection.)

The deck boat *Dolphin* is shown arriving in Broad Creek in Deltaville, Virginia, after dredging for crabs on Chesapeake Bay. The 45-foot vessel was built in 1950 by Johnny C. "Crab" Weston and his son Earl in Deltaville for Willis Wilson, Lennie Callis, and Charles Fred Montgomery, all of Deltaville. She was one of the smaller deck boats on the bay and was often used in the haul-seine fishery. (Courtesy of Willis Wilson.)

Capt. John Melvin Ward, of *Ward Bros.*, is pictured poking his head out of the pilothouse window while dredging for crabs on a cold, icy day on Chesapeake Bay in 1977. The tarp in front of the pilothouse was used to block cold air from coming through the windows. On warmer days, when the boat was being loaded with fish meal, the tarp was extended to cover the window openings to keep meal from blowing into the pilothouse. (Courtesy of Carlos Smith.)

Verna R. was built in 1948 by Charles Henry Rice of Reedville, Virginia. Rice built the boat for himself, and he worked it in Virginia's oyster- and crab-dredge fisheries. He named the boat after his second wife. Rice also constructed the 81-foot, double-deck deck boat *G.T. Forbush*, one of the larger deck boats built on the bay. (Courtesy of Edward W. Rice.)

This oyster dredge will hold 20 bushels of oysters and is used today on the deck boat *Mobjack*. The boat is used to dredge oysters on the James and York Rivers. *Mobjack* can hold 3,000 bushels of seed oysters. The boat was originally built to dredge oysters for one of the largest oyster companies in Virginia, J.H. Miles & Co. (Author's collection.)

Louisa Bush was originally 39.5 by 12.6 by 3.5 feet and was built in 1904 at Crittenden, Virginia. When she was built, the boat's gross tonnage was 10 tons. Sometime over the course of her life, she was enlarged in length and width. The *Louisa Bush* now has a gross tonnage of 20 tons and is listed at 43.5 by 13.3 by 5.1 feet in the 1994 edition of *Merchant Vessels of the United States*. When this photograph was taken in the 1970s, she was being used to dredge oysters. (Courtesy of the William C. Hight collection.)

Captains and crews of deck boats were able to work two dredges at once off of each side of the boat. The narrower, standard deadrise oyster boats were 38 to 42 feet long and allowed only one dredge to be worked off the stern. In the 1980s and 1990s, watermen started having boatbuilders create longer and wider deadrise boats to enable two dredges to be worked off the stern. Many of the larger deck boats were replaced with these more fuel-efficient deadrise boats. (Author's collection.)

The beauty of God's nature surrounding this Chesapeake Bay deck boat presents an exquisite maritime scene. On this day in December 1985, the vessel is drifting between millions of sunny spots, as the deck boat was being worked in the bay's crab-dredge fishery. This photograph was taken from the deck of *Iva W*. (Author's collection.)

The 100-foot-long *Chesapeake* was built by Lepron "Captain Lep" Johnson of Johnson Marine Railway in Crittenden, Virginia. The second-largest deck boat built on the bay, *Chesapeake* was constructed for Rufus Miles of Norfolk, Virginia, to use in planting and dredging oysters on his private oyster grounds. The vessel carried a 14-man crew and could handle four dredges in the water at one time. She was also used as an oyster buyboat and could unload eight boats at a time. When the boat was first built, *Chesapeake*'s seven-foot draft required it to be launched during the highest tide of the month, which arrived at midnight during a full moon. On that night in 1936, the community of Crittenden came down to the railway with car lights shining so everyone could see the launch. Foreman Clifton Haughwout was in charge of the construction and made the half-model used to shape the hull. He lofted *Chesapeake* on a lofting platform the size of the boat. (Courtesy of the Dr. A.L. VanName Jr. collection.)

Six

Runners and Buyboats

Deck boats are also called runners and buyboats. The term "runner" was likely first used on the bay in the early 1800s, when sailing schooners came down from Staten Island, New York, to buy oysters from Chesapeake Bay watermen. Oyster buyers would "run" oysters in their sailing vessels back to growing grounds on Long Island Sound or processing houses in New York City and Connecticut. Over time, the term "buyboat" became associated with sailing schooners, sloops, bugeyes, and—later—motorized deck boats used to buy seafood from watermen.

Early in the history of the Chesapeake Bay seafood business, watermen mostly sold seafood to customers in their own neighborhoods from hand-pulled carts or horse-drawn wagons. As demand grew on the bay for larger quantities of fish, crabs, and oysters, oyster-shucking houses, crab- and herring-processing houses, and various other seafood facilities were established within the bay region. These early plants were often some distance away from the rivers and coves where watermen were working. Buyboats, or run boats, were sent to these fishing grounds to purchase seafood from watermen.

Another type of runner is a deck boat used to tow skiffs and oystermen to private oyster grounds and back at the end of the workday; some owners of oyster plants kept a small fleet of skiffs for this purpose. Hand-tong oystermen working from the skiffs were paid piecemeal for each bushel of oysters they caught. As time passed, independent deck boat captains expanded their business by buying seed oysters from oyster tongers on James River for planting; watermelons from farmers in North Carolina to sell in Baltimore and Washington, DC; and oyster shells from shucking houses for lime plants for use in the oyster aquaculture business.

Throughout the bay region, buyboat is typically the most identifiable name for these types of boats. However, the great captains who worked the boats—such as Capt. Johnny Ward of Deltaville, Virginia; Morris Snow of Mathews County, Virginia; Jimmy Jones Belvin of Gloucester County, Virginia; and others—referred to the vessels as deck boats to denote the difference between decked over deck boats and the smaller deadrise boats without decks.

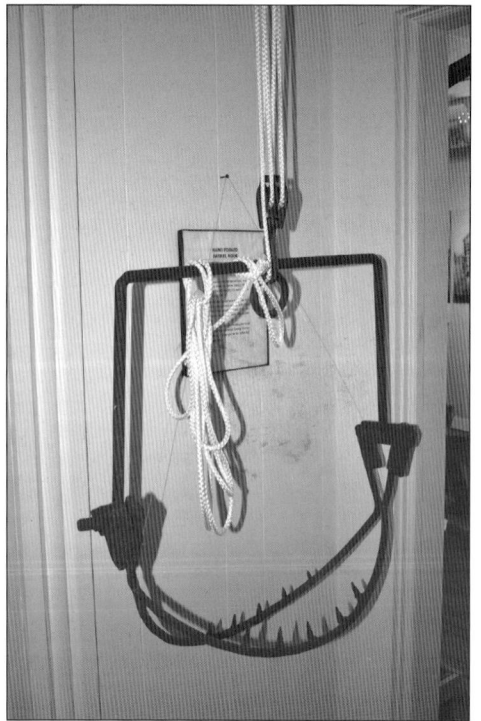

Capt. Weldon Lewis of Hoopersville, Maryland, is pictured buying hard crabs in 1954 on the deck boat *Sterling*. Lewis is buying crabs from White Stone, Virginia, crabbers Millard Boatman and Zack Ashburn at the mouths of Henry and Indian Creeks in Lancaster County, Virginia. Crabs were dumped into barrels and off-loaded from smaller workboats onto the deck of *Sterling* and hauled to crab-picking houses in Crisfield, Maryland. (Courtesy of Carroll Ashburn.)

This hand-forged barrel hook was made by blacksmith Clinton View of White Stone, Virginia, and used by Chesapeake Bay deck boat captains to hoist barrels of blue crabs onto the decks when buying crabs. The seafood business helped extend the life of the blacksmith industry even after the horseless carriage had long since taken the place of horses and their shoes. (Courtesy of the Morattico Waterfront Museum and Jack and Barbara Ashburn.)

Capt. Johnny Ward and crew are shown on the deck boat *Iva W.* buying market-size oysters in 1964 on Piankatank River. Oystermen have rafted their deadrise oyster boats off of both sides of *Iva W.* while waiting to sell their catches. Oyster buyboats have played an important role in the economic existence of the bay's oyster fishery. (Courtesy of John M. Bareford Jr.)

Hand-operated oyster tongs were introduced on the bay around 1700 and allowed oystermen to stand on a boat and grab oysters from the bottom of the bay. The oystermen pictured here would soon be selling their catch to an oyster buyboat. When a deck boat captain was willing to pay a higher price per bushel for oysters, he would hoist a flag up the mast to let tongers know they could get a better price selling to him. (Author's collection.)

Capt. Robert Dea Ailsworth is shown here atop the pilothouse keeping tally of oysters coming aboard his buyboat. Captain Ailsworth and his crew could buy oysters from four oyster boats at a time. The tallyman's job was to keep count of the number of bushels and from which boat each one came. Captain Ailsworth's deck boat, *Lillian T.*, held 1,800 bushels of oysters. The business of buying oysters was a cash-and-carry business. There were often large sums of money on boats. Some buyboat captains kept the money in a small safe, and most kept a loaded pistol nearby to discourage robbers. Oystermen shoveled their own oysters into the tub, also called a measure. Some watermen are extremely talented in cribbing the measure—using the shovel, they stack the oysters so most of them are standing upright in the tub, taking up more space and cutting the buyboat captain out of a full measure of oysters. Another element of the tallyman's job was to monitor the cribbing. (Courtesy of Alfred E. Ailsworth Jr.)

This oyster tally sheet speaks to the way buyboat captains kept track of the number of bushels of seed oyster purchased from each vessel. Each boat is given a number, and each bushel is given a mark. When they get to five bushels, it is a tally. This load of seed oysters was purchased in 1959 on James River by Capt. George Dungan on the buyboat *Mitchell*. The seed was purchased for planter Carter Arnest of Mount Holly, Virginia. Dungan purchased 1,695 bushels that day. Some buyboat captains keep the tally on a 6-by-12-inch tally board made of wood with a pencil tied to a string attached to the board. When they finished the day's tally, they used a block of wood with sandpaper wrapped around it to sand off the tally marks and prepare for the next day of buying. (Courtesy of George B. Dungan Jr.)

Addison Lombard Carter ran a general merchandise store in 1868 in Monaskon, Virginia, and provided printed money to local oystermen for store credit in exchange for oysters they caught. Carter was also in the oyster-packing and bulk shipping trade. During the Reconstruction era, when currency was short, he printed his own money. He owned a schooner and a bugeye that he used to buy oysters and to haul freight. (Courtesy of Louise Jesse.)

Oysterman Ben Wormeley is shown unloading oysters from the deck boat *Grace* in the 1940s at J.W. Hurley Seafood in Urbanna, Virginia. The tub used to hold the oysters is called a Virginia measure, which holds a little over a bushel of oysters. Oystermen were paid a certain amount per measure. *Grace* was owned by Capt. Clyde Green and homeported on Lagrange Creek on Rappahannock River. (Courtesy of the Jonesey Payne collection.)

Hawsie B. was built by Linwood Price at Deltaville, Virginia, in 1932. This photograph was taken in Crisfield, Maryland, when ice had made up in the harbor. *Hawsie B.* had a safe aboard her that was used to hold stock money for buying oysters and fish. *Hawsie B.* was used to buy oysters and herring for a fish-cutting house. The herring were gutted, and after their heads were cut off, they were placed in brine to make pickled herring. (Courtesy of the William C. Hight collection; photograph by Barbara Thomas.)

The deck boat *Dora Estelle* is moored in Cambridge, Maryland, where she was being used as an oyster buyboat. *Dora Estelle* was built in Ewell, Maryland, on Smith Island by Noah T. Evans in 1923. She was owned by Charles Irving Henderson of Crisfield and, later, by Dewy Evans of Tangier Island. (Author's collection.)

Tangier Island, Virginia, was home port to numerous Chesapeake Bay deck boats. This 1949 photograph of Tangier Harbor shows the magnitude of the island's dependency on wooden boats. For generations, Tangier Island residents have been some of the most prolific watermen on the bay. Tangier Island watermen purchased crabs, fish, and oysters and supplied seafood to processing houses in Crisfield, Maryland, and Cape Charles, Virginia. (Courtesy of Lewis Parks.)

After the Civil War, when enslaved people were granted their freedom, Chesapeake Bay and its rivers, creeks, and coves provided sustenance for newly freed African Americans. During oyster season, buyboat captains paid hard cash for oysters regardless of who harvested them. Over time, African Americans were able to use these resources to purchase land, build homes, and improve their quality of life, which positively impacted generations of families. (Courtesy of J.D. Davis.)

Maryland's sailing skipjack fleet relied on motorized buyboats to purchase their oysters and take their catch to market. This photograph, taken in November 1958, shows four skipjacks selling to an oyster buyboat. Maryland law prevents motorized vessels from dredging oysters in the state's waters. A dredge can only be worked in Maryland waters on a boat powered by wind and sail. This has resulted in the preservation of the only commercial-fishing sailing fleet in North America. Maryland's state legislature named the deadrise skipjack the official state boat in 1958. This style of vessel is revered by maritime historians and the general public. The hulls of skipjacks and motorized deck boats are built using the same deadrise and cross-planked-bottom style. (Courtesy of Chesapeake Bay Maritime Museum.)

Ruby Chrystal was built in Crittenden, Virginia, by Capt. Lep Johnson in 1924. The vessel is shown on the rails at Alton Smith's railway in Horn Harbor, Virginia. *Ruby Chrystal* was used as an oyster buyboat and a crab-dredge boat. Johnson was one of just a few builders on the Chesapeake who constructed his V-bottoms with the planking laid stem-to-stern. Most bay deck boats have cross-planked bottoms. (Courtesy of Mildred Stillman.)

The small flag attached to the rigging of the oyster buyboat *Grace* indicates that Capt. Clyde Green of Remlik, Virginia, way paying more for a bushel of oysters than the other buyboats on that day. In this picture taken at the oyster house on Lagrange Creek, mate Dick Burrell is on the bow securing the lines on *Grace*. (Courtesy of Marie Green Stallings.)

Eddie Abbott of Water View, Virginia, had Linwood and Milford Price of Deltaville, Virginia, build *Marie* in 1950. The boat is named for Eddie's wife, Marie Abbott. Abbott used the boat to buy oysters on Rappahannock and James Rivers. He owned and operated Water View Packing Co., where his oysters were shucked and prepared for market. (Courtesy of the Jonesey Payne collection.)

In this photograph, *Marie* is in her final stages of life, as the vessel has been laid up for years in a shallow cove in Lancaster County, Virginia. With the tide rising and falling inside her hull, her days are numbered. This is the fate of many of the grand old wooden boats of Chesapeake Bay. (Author's collection.)

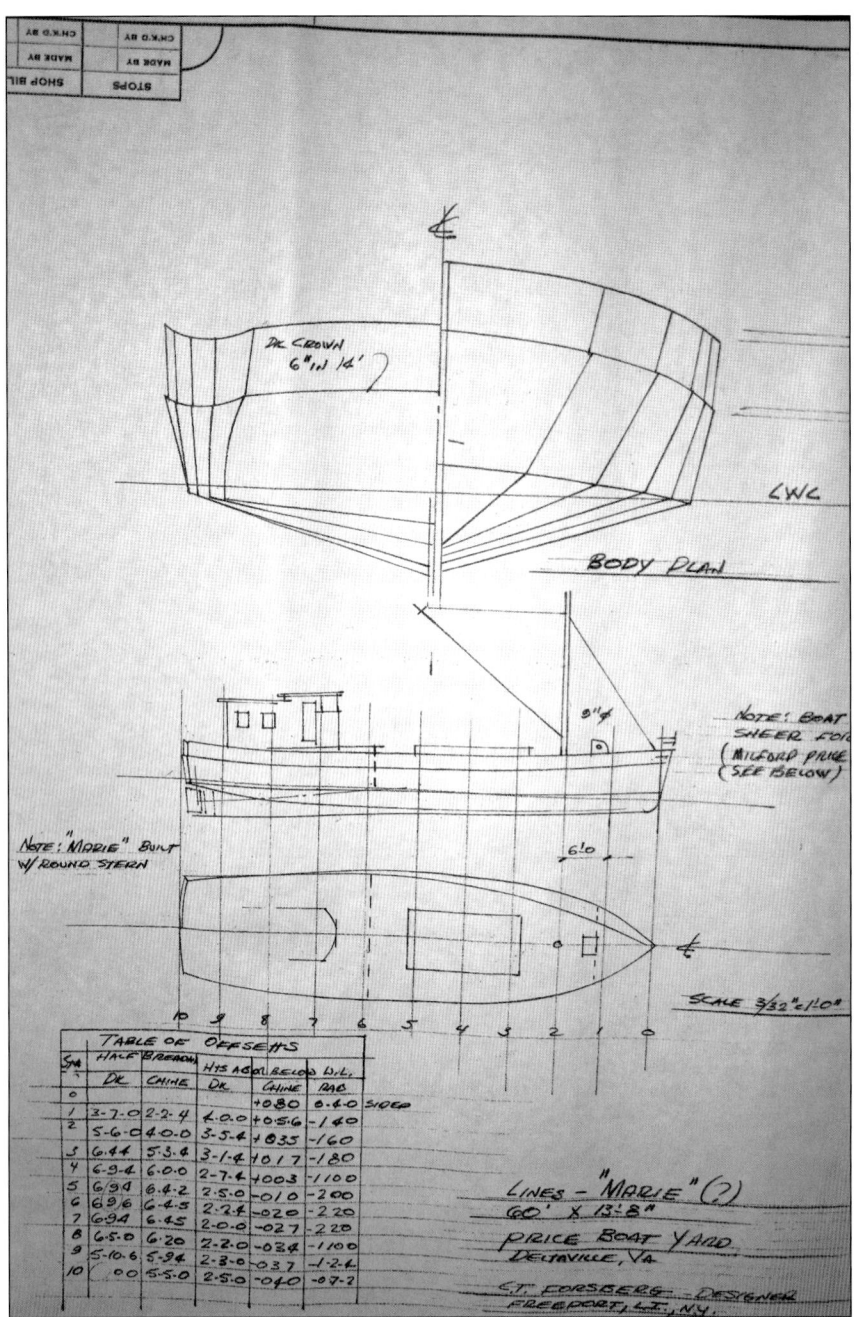

Most Chesapeake Bay deadrise wooden boats were built using a "rack of eye" method—without plans. The 60-foot-long deck boat *Marie* was one of just a few deck boats designed by naval architect C.T. Forsberg. The boat was designed in 1950 for Deltaville boatbuilders Linwood and Milford Price. After building *Marie*, the Prices had architect Harry Bulifant revise the plan for him to build 58-foot standard deadrise hulls. Since most deck boats were built using rack of eye, these written plans for *Marie* are extremely rare. In addition to buying oysters on the river, Eddie Abbott and his family used *Marie* for entertainment and, in the summertime, held large family and neighborhood picnics on the boat. (Courtesy of Joe Conboy.)

Seven

Pound-Net and Haul-Seine Boats

The haul seine and pound net are two forms of gear used on Chesapeake Bay that require a fairly large labor force for installing gear and nets. Over the years, these styles of gear enabled watermen to harvest large quantities of fish. This encouraged fishermen to invest in building deck boats for use in these types of fisheries.

The smallest deck boats built on the bay were used in the haul-seine fishery. Sweet little haul-seine boats ranged from 38 to 40 feet in length and had 3 to 3.5 feet of draft. Haul-seine nets are worked close to shore and require the use of small, shallow-draft deck boats. The haul seine was introduced from England by early settlers. The modern deck boat came into play in 1938, when Earl Hudgins of Mathews County invented the purse pocket. This enabled fishermen to trap a school of fish in a pocket within the net and close the pocket so fish could not escape. The deck boat is used to haul the pocket full of fish out into deep water. Once the boat is in deeper water, fish are bailed from the net with a dip net into the hold of the deck boat.

The pound-net fishery requires a larger boat ranging from 55 to 65 feet in length. A larger platform is needed for hauling and installing 40- to 80-foot-long pound-net poles into the bottom of the bay and for working nets in dangerous, deeper waters. The pound net was introduced on the Chesapeake in 1858 by Capt. Henry Fitzgerald, but the gear was not extensively used by bay watermen until the 1870s.

Around 1870, George Snediker of Gravesend, Long Island, New York, and Charles Doughty of Fairhaven, New Jersey, came to the region and set up shop on the banks of the James River a few miles above its mouth. They were successful in establishing a fishery, and it spread throughout the bay region. The boats in this fishery are often referred to as trap boats, and pound nets are sometimes called trap nets. Hundreds of deck boats were built for the bay's pound-net fishery.

Ellen Marie is a classic pound-net, or trap, boat built in 1925. Some trap boats were not originally built as deck boats. In this photograph, one can see that the pilothouse sits on the ceiling or floor of *Ellen Marie*. She was later decked over, with the pilothouse raised to sit on top of a deck, and rebuilt into a traditional deck boat. (Courtesy of Thomas E. Owens.)

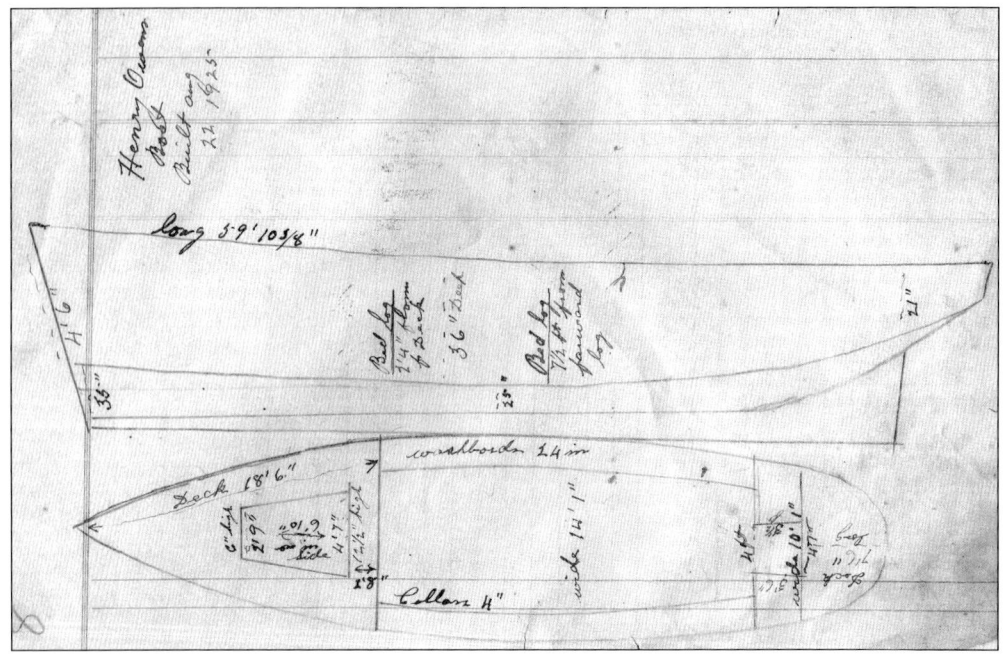

Ellen Marie was built in 1925 by Lennie and Alton Smith for pound-net fisherman Henry Owens of Mathews County, Virginia. This rare drawing of *Ellen Marie* was done by the Smiths before the boat was built to give Owens an understanding of what his boat would look like. This also gave the owner an opportunity to provide input into what he wanted built into his new boat. (Courtesy of Mildred Stillman.)

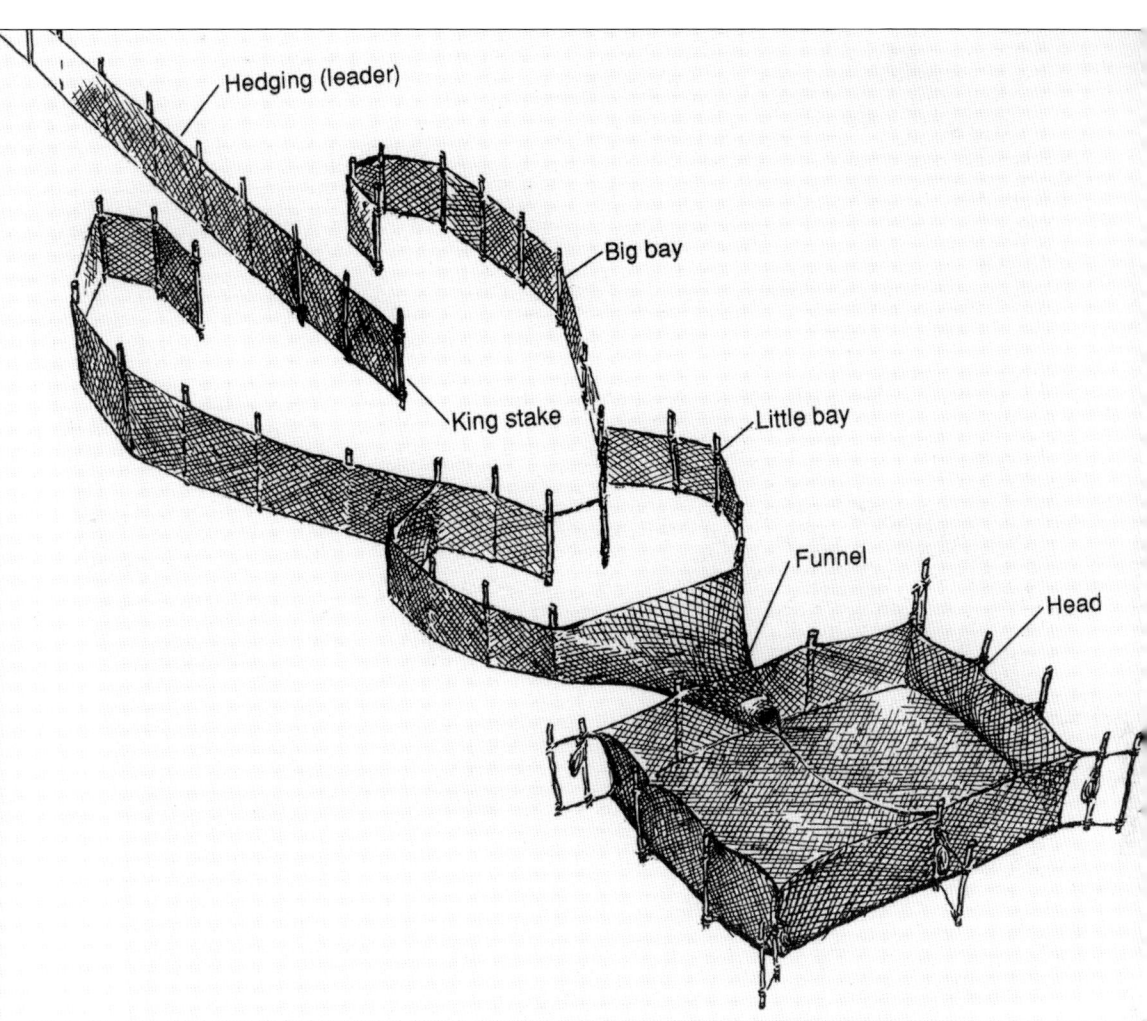

The pound net was introduced on Chesapeake Bay in 1858 but had little impact until the 1880s. During the last two decades of the 19th century and the first half of the 20th century, use of the net spread from one end of the bay to the other. Large boats were required to install pound poles and carry large and heavy payloads of fish to market. Many Virginia and Maryland deck boats were specifically built to work in the pound-net fishery. This photograph shows a modern-style pound net similar to what is used today. When the pound net was first introduced, early pioneers in the fishery met strong resistance from local fishermen. However, the pound net eventually caught on and became one of the main styles of gear used to harvest finfish. (Courtesy of the Virginia Institute of Marine Science.)

Herman M. Krentz was built for the bay's pound net fishery and was owned by pound-netters Grover and Hiram Lewis and, later, by fisherman Ryland Gaskins. The vessel spent most of its working life in that fishery. The boat was well-known in the Reedville area and, although it is long since gone, the pilothouse was restored and is a nautical centerpiece on the grounds of the Reedville Fishermen's Museum. (Courtesy of George and Becky Butler.)

This James River 25-foot shad net fishing bateau is typical of early boats used to fish shad. The vessel is not a deck boat but is a forerunner to the modern deck boat and has features associated with the larger deck boats. Most notable is the house positioned near the stern. Workboats are designed to accommodate the needs of the fishermen. The space forward of the engine and house is there to provide an open area to work nets and carry payload. (Author's photo.)

It took the power of Capt. Eddie Gaskins and his four-man crew to set and drive pound-net poles into the bottom of the bay when setting them in the spring. The pine poles were cut from forest in Northumberland County and dragged out of the wood by a horse. In 1989, the horse, Midnight, owned by Ralph Thompson of Brown Store, Virginia, was still being used to drag large pine poles out of the woods. (Author's collection.)

George P. Butler of Reedville, Virginia, maintained many of the Chesapeake Bay deck boats on Virginia's Northern Neck at Reedville Marine Railway on Main Street. When he died in 1976, his son George M. Butler continued to haul and maintain deck boats. Local railways played a significant role in keeping the wooden boats of Chesapeake Bay maintained and in working order. (Courtesy of George and Becky Butler.)

The pile driver, as shown here near the mast on *Ellen Marie*, was a main tool used by bay watermen to drive pound-net poles into the bottom of the bay. After the poles were positioned and driven down, the pile driver was removed from the boat so the vessel could be used to carry fish from the net to processing houses. Mauls and various other apparatuses were designed to drive poles into the river and bay bottoms. (Courtesy of Thomas E. Owens.)

Maid King was built in 1922 and used in Virginia's pound-net fishery by the late Shelly Rowe of Gwynn's Island, Virginia. The vessel is not a deck boat but is a good example of the type of open boat large enough to be converted into a deck boat. A pile driver is mounted near the bow, and the vessel has a classic outside, sailboat-style tiller/rudder system for steering. She was never converted into a deck boat. (Author's collection.)

Gilbert H. was built in 1938 by L.R. and Alton Smith for fisherman Boyd Hall of Mathews County, Virginia. She is another example of a boat built as an open trap boat and later decked over. The completed 48-foot hull cost $700, plus $50 for the pilothouse. Hall installed a 65-horsepower Bridgeport engine that cost $500. He paid the $1,250 for the boat and motor in cash. The boat was named after his son and later renamed *Icylene III* in the 1970s. (Courtesy of Sandy Hall Diggs.)

Manfred L. was built in Denbigh, Virginia, in 1922 and, for many years, used to haul freight. In 2002, Gaskins Seafood of Ophelia, Virginia, owned the vessel and used her in Maryland's Potomac River pound-net fishery. This photograph shows the boat loaded down with pound poles ready to be set. It also shows brakes installed on the sides of *Manfred L.* that hold the poles. Once all of the poles are set, the brakes are removed from the boat. When pound nets were being fished in deep water, fishermen needed large deck boats (at least 55 feet long) to carry long poles out to the fishing grounds. The 38-foot *Manfred L.* was long enough for Gaskins' poles, which were being driven into 20 feet of water. Today, Virginia and Maryland pound nets are set in relatively shallow water. The amount of manpower needed to set a deepwater net, the cost of nets and poles, and reduced catches of fish have made it not cost-effective for fishermen to work nets in deep water. (Author's collection.)

Deck boats were the primary platform used to haul the poles used in setting pound nets. However, as fishermen began setting nets in shallower waters and using shorter and lighter poles, some switched to using smaller boats to transport poles. The deadrise boat *Joyce*, pictured here, is an example of one of these smaller boats—and an example of lost work for the larger deck boats, which were also more expensive to operate. (Author's collection)

This photograph shows a deepwater Chesapeake Bay pound net being hauled to the surface by a 12-man crew. The men are working out of a large skiff referred to as a tow-bat in some areas of Virginia. A tow-bat, or pound-net skiff, is towed to the fishing grounds behind a deck boat. The men working the pound net often sang as they worked; this was a way to pass the time and coordinate everyone pulling together. (Courtesy of Thomas E. Owens.)

Bobbie was used in the Potomac River pound-net fishery. The skiff tied alongside *Bobbie* has a whiskered bow fender made of rope, a battery-powered wench on the bow deck used to haul in lines, and becket lines hanging from the side of the skiff—these were used to tie off the net when hauling it to the surface. (Author's collection.)

The hold of *Martha Virginia* is loaded with spot fish caught in a Potomac River pound net. *Martha Virginia* was built in 1940 in Deltaville, Virginia, for Vernon W. Crockett of Tangier Island. This photograph shows the bail, or dip, net used to bail fish from the pound-net pocket and transfer it into the fishhold of the deck boat. (Author's collection.)

Martha Virginia was modified for the pound-net fishery to have a short stump cabin aft, which allowed for more payload and work space forward of the cabin. When it was built, the vessel had a traditional pilothouse and was used for buying oysters and freighting. When the boat was used in the pound-net fishery, it was worked daily without overnight stays and had no real use for a large cabin. (Author's collection.)

This is an extremely rare photograph of a V-stern, or diamond-stern, deck boat. *Elizabeth D.* was built by Alton and Lennie Smith of Mathews County, Virginia, in 1927. The stern style evolved from the double-ended V-bow and V-stern built into sail-powered log canoes. A V-stern deck boat was used in the bay's clam fishery, where fishermen often worked stern to sea, and in the haul-seine fishery, where a net was sometimes brought in over the stern. (Courtesy of Mildred Stillman.)

This image shows the deck boat *Dudley* moored at Fred Biddlecomb's fish house in Northumberland County, Virginia. The tall, enclosed building on the shore was used for the storage of nets and gear during the off-season and for cold storage of fish during the working season. The shorter, open building to the left of the enclosed building was used daily to off-load, cull, and box fish. (Author's collection.)

Linda Carol, originally named *Croaker*, was built in 1931 by Alton and Lennie Smith of Mathews County. The Smiths built numerous deck boats for the bay's pound-net fishery. The father/son boatbuilding team first worked on Pepper Creek in Mathews County and later crafted vessels at Port Haywood, Virginia, also in Mathews County. The Smiths were pioneers in the development of deadrise and cross-planked construction on Chesapeake Bay. (Courtesy of Michaela Chowning.)

This photograph shows how a pound net is fished. The men standing in the skiff at left have hauled the pocket full of fish to the surface. The fish pocket and fish are positioned between the tow-bat and deck boat. An engine on the deck boat is used to lower and raise the dip net. Here, the dip net has been lowered into the fish pocket and has brought up a net full of fish. The two men standing on the deck are holding ropes tied to the dip net; these help them guide the dip net up and over the fishhold. When the bottom of the dip net is opened, the fish fall into the hold. After the pound-net pocket is completely empty of fish, the deck boat motors the catch to a fish house, where the payload is off-loaded at the dock. (Courtesy of Thomas E. Owens.)

Dudley was built in 1938 by Gilbert White of Palmer, Virginia. She was used for many years in Virginia's pound-net fishery and built for and owned by the Biddlecomb family of Reedville until 2018. Until his death, Fred M. Biddlecomb worked *Dudley* in the pound-net fishery and ran her as a charter fishing boat. She is named *Dudley* for Fred's older brother. (Author's collection.)

In this photograph, *Dudley* is rigged for pound-net fishing. A dip net—used for hauling fish out of the fish pocket—is lashed to the rigging near the mast. Note that there is a forepeak hatch on the shore that most likely came off of a deck boat. *Dudley* was built by Gilbert White, who started his professional boatbuilding career by constructing log canoes in Mathews County, Virginia. (Courtesy of Joe Conboy.)

Peggy was built in 1925 by Harry A. Hudgins of Peary, Virginia, for pound-net fisherman Walter Burroughs of New Point, Virginia. The boat, named for Burroughs's daughter, was originally built as an open boat and was later decked over. She was later owned (and worked until 1994) by pound-net fisherman Edward Grinnell. In this picture, *Peggy*, which is now owned by the Mathews Maritime Foundation and Museum, is being painted and polished for the upcoming boating season. Disregarding the vehicle parked beside *Peggy* and the modern ladders at right, this picture of a deck boat on the hard could have been taken most anywhere on the bay in the first half of the 20th century. (Author's collection.)

Thomas E. was built in 1948 by Alton Smith for Henry Owens to use in the bay's pound-net and crab-dredge fisheries. When this photograph was taken in the 1950s, the deck boat was being used in the bay's pound-net fishery. The skiff behind Thomas E. was used by fishermen as a platform to stand on while they hauled the net full of fish up to the surface. (Courtesy of Thomas E. Owens.)

This tow-bat was used in the pound-net fishery. If there were just a few fish in a net, rather than bailing the fish into the hold of the deck boat, the catch was dropped into the skiff and towed back to home port. If there was a large amount of fish, the skiff was used to bail fish into the hold of the deck boat, as shown in the photograph on page 94. The bow fender attached to the bow is made from an old automobile tire. (Author's collection.)

The fishhold of the 60-foot deck boat *Seven Brothers* is shown here full of fish as she cruises through rough seas. *Seven Brothers* was built in 1928 by Gilbert White and used in the deepwater bay pound-net fishery. She was later rigged and used in the bay's menhaden snapper-rig fishery. The vessel could hold 110,000 menhaden. (Courtesy of Roland George.)

Once a boat is back at the dock, the fish are culled and boxed. In this photograph, spot fish are being dumped onto a culling station at Eddie Gaskins' dock in Ophelia, Virginia. The fish are being off-loaded from the fishhold of *Martha Virginia*. At the time this photograph was taken in the 1980s, Gaskins owned three deck boats: *Martha Virginia*, *Bobbie*, and *Manfred L.* Today, Gaskins and his sons no longer own deck boats and no longer fish pound nets. The family, however, still fishes for a living by using gill nets. (Author's collection.)

The 102-year-old *Ella K.* is shown on the rails at Smith Marine Railway in Dare, Virginia, in 2015. The 50-foot deck boat was built in 1918 by James Smith of Perrin, Virginia, and used in the pound-net, crab-dredge, and haul-seine fisheries. She was one of the last deck boats still being worked in the winter crab-dredge fishery in 2008, the last season before the winter fishery was closed by the state. (Author's collection.)

Pound-net fishermen Grover and Hiram Lewis of Reedville, Virginia, had Herman M. Krentz build this 55-foot deck boat in 1928 at Kayan, Virginia. Hiram's daughter Marian Lewis is standing in the pilothouse door. The boat was named after the builder. Krentz built the sailing skipjack *H.M. Krentz*, which was also named after him, in 1955. After moving from Kayan, he built the skipjack at his new boat shop in Harryhogan, Virginia. (Courtesy of George M. and Becky Butler.)

Reedville Fishermen's Museum saved the original pilothouse of *Herman M. Krentz* and has made it into a centerpiece on the grounds of the museum. The museum has carefully maintained the pilothouse, leaving it in the state it was in when *Herman M. Krentz* was being used as a pound-net boat. (Author's collection.)

The deck boat *Herman M. Krentz* was powered by twin engines and had a separate clutch for each engine. Two clutch handles are visible in this photograph—one is in the foreground of the photograph, and the other is near the molding of the far door. The wheel and paneling inside the pilothouse are original to the structure. (Author's collection.)

This compass used by Grover and Hiram Lewis, fishermen and the former owners of *Herman M. Krentz*, is still mounted in the pilothouse. A compass, barometer (referred to by bay fishermen as a glass), and a lead line were three tools used by deck boat captains for navigation and to determine weather conditions. A lead line is a long rope knotted every three feet with a piece of lead tied to the bottom; it was used to determine water depth. (Author's collection.)

A pilothouse usually had two bunks—for the captain and mate. Most boats had the galley situated in the rear of the pilothouse. The forepeak was used to accommodate crew. Some deck boats had sleeping quarters built into the forepeak, and some boats had the galley in the forepeak. (Author's collection.)

The deck boat pictured at left in this photograph was used by Willis and Obie Wilson of Deltaville in Virginia's haul-seine fishery. One year, they caught a dolphin and sent a boy out into the neighborhood to tell people. When the curious citizens started coming to the dock, Obie stopped them at the shore and charged each person a nickel to see the fish. They had 160 people come and made $8. (Courtesy of Willis Wilson.)

Seven Brothers is shown loaded down with menhaden at a dock on the Northern Neck of Virginia. The vessel sank off Stingray Point on the Rappahannock River in 2001, ending her 83 years on Chesapeake Bay. When this photograph was taken in May 1984, Capt. Roland George was working Seven Brothers in the menhaden snapper-rig fishery. (Courtesy of Roland George.)

The deck boat *Dudley* and deadrise *Mary Trew* were owned by the Biddlecomb family of Reedville, Virginia, and used in Potomac River and Chesapeake Bay pound-net fisheries. The boats were crafted by boatbuilder Gilbert White. When White built *Dudley* in 1938, the Biddlecomb family supplied the dressed lumber and keel log for the job. White was paid $550 for his labor. White was an old-fashioned builder who would go into the woods and find a tree shaped just right for a knee (frame) and cut it on the spot. When chopping was required, he used a hatchet and a woodpile axe. He learned the trade from log-canoe builders in Mathews County and created all his boats using what hand tools he had. (Author's collection.)

The evolution of gasoline engines played a major role in the development of bay deck boats. As engines grew in horsepower, boats became more efficient in the fishery or trade in which they were utilized. This 1916 Mianus Motor Works catalog of secondhand motors was passed down from C.P. Garrett of Bowlers Wharf, Virginia, to his grandson Wit Garrett. The largest engine in the catalog is a 27-horsepower Pierce-Arrow. The second-largest is an 18-horsepower Grant-Ferris. Other brands of engines in the catalog include Knox, Lozier, Ardmore, Lathrop, Maine, Stevens, Metz & Weiss, Oriole, Sagamore, Palmer, Ferro, Blomstrom, Toppan, Winkley, Essex, Fairbanks, Hubbard, and Rapid. Any of these brands could have been found on pre-1920 deck boats. (Courtesy of Wit Garrett.)

Eight

PLEASURE AND EDUCATION BOATS

As commercial fishing and freighting declined on the bay, preservationists and deck boat enthusiasts have saved some of the old boats and turned them into recreational yachts and education boats. With the insertion of a truck cabin over the fishhold hatch, additional headroom space can be added to accommodate comfortable living quarters. Some private restorations of boats have had costs in the six-figure range. Museums and nonprofit organizations have also saved vessels by restoring boats to promote and teach environmental studies and the heritage and culture of the bay to both students and the general public.

With the decline of the bay's boatbuilding culture, it is becoming harder to find boatyards that can properly maintain the vessels. Several museums have established their own boat shops and have either purchased or built traditional marine railways to haul and maintain their boats.

The Chesapeake Bay Maritime Museum in St. Michaels, Maryland, has its own side-by-side railway and boat shop. The boatyard is conveniently laid out for educational tours and to teach visitors about the construction of wooden boats. The museum owns and maintains two deck boats, *Old Point* and *Winnie Estelle*.

Calvert Marine Museum in Solomons, Maryland, has *William B. Tennison*, the last surviving deck boat converted from sail and still operating on the bay. The craft is a nine-logged bugeye built in 1899 by Frank Laird of Crabb Island, Maryland.

The Deltaville Maritime Museum in Deltaville, Virginia, owns and maintains the log deck boat *F.D. Crockett*; Mathews Maritime Foundation and Museum in Mathews, Virginia, owns the boat *Peggy*; Echo Hill Outdoor School in Betterton, Maryland, owns the deck boat *Annie D.*; Reedville Fishermen's Museum in Reedville, Virginia, owns the boat *Elva C.*; and the Living Classrooms Foundation, with locations in Baltimore and Washington, DC, has *Mildred Belle*.

In 2004, deck boat owners from all across the bay formed the Chesapeake Bay Buyboat Association. The association holds an annual buyboat rendezvous at waterfront towns and cities throughout the bay, and the public is encouraged to come and view the boats and learn about their history.

The *Iva W.* was built in 1929 by John Wright of Deltaville, Virginia, for Capt. Johnny Ward. Captain Johnny worked the boat until he retired in the 1990s. He used it for planting seed oysters; buying oysters; running watermelons from Edenton, North Carolina, to Baltimore, Maryland; and dredging crabs in Virginia's winter crab-dredge fishery. In 1998, the boat left the Ward family and was converted to a double deckhouse luxury yacht. It is now owned by Scott Bessette of Washington, DC. (Author's collection.)

In June 2019, the deck boat *Linda Carol* was saved from a fire by the York County Fire and Life Safety fire/rescue boat. *Linda Carol* was moored in a slip next to the Surf Rider Restaurant in Poquoson, Virginia, when the restaurant caught fire and was totally destroyed. In this photograph, *Linda Carol* is shown at Marina Cove Boat Basin in Hampton, Virginia, where the extent of the damage was being determined. Owner Bill Mullis and boatbuilder David Rollins meticulously restored the boat in 2016. (Author's collection.)

Emmitt H. is owned by Wesley Sanger of Peary, Virginia, and was built in 1947. At 37 feet long, the vessel is one of the smallest deck boats on the bay. This photograph was taken at the 2011 Chesapeake Bay Buyboat Rendezvous on Tangier Island, Virginia. Sanger, his family, and their dog regularly attend the annual rendezvous. (Author's collection.)

Elva C. was built by Gilbert White in 1922. The boat is owned by the Reedville Fishermen's Museum and is used as an education boat. This photograph was taken in October 2001, when the boat was being used to carry museum members out to view the annual Turkey Shoot Regatta in Rappahannock River. (Courtesy of Tom Chillemi.)

In this 2004 photograph, *East Hampton* and *Ellen Marie* are en route to the first Chesapeake Bay Buyboat Rendezvous in Rock Hall, Maryland. At the time, *East Hampton* was owned by David and Trudy Rollins of Poquoson, Virginia, and *Ellen Marie* was owned by Paul Vrooman of Mathews County. (Courtesy of Hannah Straub.)

The deck boat *Mundy Point* was built in 1929 by Gilbert White and originally named *Lawson*. When this picture was taken in 1992, *Mundy Point* was in the course of being converted to a yacht. While renovation was underway, a plastic covering was built over the deck to keep rain out of the hull. David and Sheila Carr of Reedville meticulously worked to make the vessel into a home on the water. After living on the boat for nearly 30 years, they recently sold it. (Courtesy of David and Sheila Carr.)

Samuel M. Bailey was built by Garner Gibson in 1957 as an oyster buyboat. It is now owned by Steve Bailey of Bushwood, Maryland, and has been converted into a yacht. In the 1960s, owner Sam Bailey would buy as many as 3,000 bushels of market-size oysters from watermen from October 15—the first day of oyster season—to Christmas. (Author's collection.)

Weekend picnic cruises on sailing vessels—and, later, on motor-powered deck boats—were exciting events for young and old. Cigarettes and Regent starched men's shirt collars are visible in this early-20th-century photograph of a group of young people enjoying a Sunday cruise on the Rappahannock River. (Courtesy of Middlesex County Museum.)

R.E. Roberts stands on the deck of Big *Muriel Eileen* at the start of a weekend excursion to Tangier Island. As the owner of Lord-Mott Company, a vegetable- and oyster-canning firm based in Baltimore, Maryland, and Urbanna, Virginia, Roberts used *Muriel Eileen* for hauling freight and canned products from his factories. At least once each summer, he used the boat for a weeklong family cruise on the bay. Awnings were installed to provide shade, comfortable chairs were brought aboard, and food fit for a wealthy businessman and his family was prepared each day in the galley. Roberts often invited friends and employees to go along on trips. He demanded that the boat be in tip-top condition when he and his family set foot on it and, while cruising the bay, the captain and mates were supplied uniforms to dress the part. Big *Muriel Eileen* was built in 1926 by J.W. Smith of Bena, Virginia. (Courtesy of George Mills.)

Pictured during a pleasure trip to Tangier Island with the R.E. Roberts family in the 1930s, Virginia "Tootsie" Mills sits on the upper deck rails of Big *Muriel Eileen*. Virginia's husband, Earle, managed the Lord-Mott Company in Urbanna, Virginia, from 1930 until it closed in 1976. Roberts owned Big *Muriel Eileen*, and a perk of working for him was the opportunity to enjoy a summer cruise on the bay. (Courtesy of George Mills.)

Elsie Louise was used to haul freight and buy oysters, but on occasion, the vessel was used to carry family and friends on fishing and day-cruising trips. The family members in this photograph appear to be dressed in their Sunday best and had likely been out on an afternoon cruise. (Courtesy of Joe Cardwell.)

Veteran is owned by Mike and Holly Sheffield of Urbanna, Virginia. They own Golden Age Charters and carry passengers on sunrise and sunset tours. The hull of *Veteran* is the original hull of *Elsie Louise* built in 1914 in Irvington, Virginia, by J. Wood Tull. (Author's collection.)

Coastal Queen was built in Hudson, Maryland, in 1928 and originally named *A.G. Price*. *A.G. Price* was used as an oyster buyboat and was converted in 1958 into a double-decker yacht and renamed *Coastal Queen*. The boat received national acclaim in 1965 when it was included in a book called *The Inside Passage* by Anthony Bailey. The book is about a trip down the Atlantic Intracoastal Waterway aboard *Coastal Queen*. (Author's collection.)

In this image, the deck boats Big *Muriel Eileen* and *Elsie Louise* are moored at J.W. Hurley and Son oyster house on Urbanna Creek. The boats are being used as platforms for people to watch the annual Urbanna Labor Day Boat Race Regatta. The event ran from 1939 to 1966, and deck boats provided spectators with a close-up view of the races. The event started by featuring sailboat races and transitioned to include outboard and inboard powerboat racing. (Courtesy of Anne Wheeley.)

Annie D. (Drewer) was built in 1957 for Vernon Drewer by Johnny "Big Johnny" C. Weston of Deltaville, Virginia. Thomas Asbury Pruitt of Tangier Island later owned the boat and used it as an oyster buyboat. The vessel was donated to the Echo Hill Outdoor School in Worton, Maryland, in 1983. It was restored in 1985 and is now used by the school as an education vessel. (Author's collection.)

When this photograph of *Annie D.* was taken in 2004, the vessel was entering the Rock Hall, Maryland, harbor to attend the first Chesapeake Bay Buyboat Rendezvous. The annual rendezvous is held at different waterfront communities in Maryland and Virginia. The main purpose of the rendezvous is to promote the heritage and culture of the boats. (Courtesy of Hannah Straub.)

Bessie L. is owned by Andy Newman and moored in Rock Hall, Maryland. She was a showpiece at the 2019 Chesapeake Bay Buyboat Rendezvous in Chestertown, Maryland. *Bessie L.*, one of the newest boats in the fleet, was built in 1994 by Edgar Jenkins of Gloucester County, Virginia. The boat is named after the original *Bessie L.*, which was built in 1923 by Linwood Price of Deltaville. (Author's collection.)

Paul Pruitt had *P.E. Pruitt* built in 1925 in Crisfield, Maryland. The vessel has been meticulously converted into a yacht, and each year, owners Kevin and Ilona Flynn attend the Chesapeake Bay Buyboat Rendezvous. When Paul had the boat built in Crisfield, he requested a "common" square stern be built onto the boat. When the boat was completed, he hired Deltaville builder Linwood Price to build him a "pretty" round stern, which is still on the boat today. (Author's collection.)

Thomas J. is owned by Tom Parker of Rolph's Wharf, Maryland. She was built in 1948 by J.S. Jenkins of Gloucester County, Virginia. The vessel has been converted into a yacht and is pictured here in 2016 during the Chesapeake Bay Buyboat Rendezvous at the Oyster Farm Marina in Cape Charles, Virginia. (Courtesy of Michaela Chowning.)

East Hampton of Chestertown, Maryland, was built in 1925 by Freeman Hudgins and Boney Diggs in Mathews County, Virginia. She was originally an open boat built with a V-shaped stern and used in Virginia's pound-net fishery. She was rebuilt and converted to a deck boat with a round stern by Frank Smith of Perrin, Virginia. Benny Williams Jr. of Gloucester County, Virginia, was dredging crabs in her in 1999 when boatwright David Rollins of Poquoson, Virginia, bought the boat and converted it into a yacht. Rollins and his wife, Trudy, cruised the bay for many years before selling the boat to Barry K. Buckley. The boat is homeported on the Chester River. (Author's collection.)

Georgie E. was built by Alton Smith in 1944 in Susan, Virginia. The vessel was later renamed *Captain Latane*. When it was rebuilt and converted to a yacht in 2015 by Eyre Baldwin of Cape Charles, the boat reverted to its original name. This photograph was taken at the 2016 Chesapeake Bay Buyboat Rendezvous in Cape Charles. (Courtesy of Michaela Chowning.)

55th Virginia was built in Deltaville, Virginia, by Ed and Billy Norton and Grover Lee Owens in 1971. This was the last deck boat built in Deltaville, where hundreds of deck boats had been built in the 1920s, 1930s, and 1940s. *55th Virginia* is owned by William "Bill" C. Hight of Urbanna, Virginia, who converted the deck boat into a yacht and cruiser. The vessel is named after the Confederate division that Hight's great-great-grandfather William S. Christian commanded in the Civil War. (Courtesy of Michaela Chowning.)

PropWash was built in 1925 by Linwood Price of Deltaville, Virginia, for John Sterling of Crisfield. The boat was converted into a yacht by owners David and Brenda Wright of Dumfries, Virginia. Over the course of its life, *PropWash* has had four names. The boat was originally named *Agnes Sterling* in 1925. It was renamed *Wayne Christy* in 1966, *Old Squaw* in 1990, and *PropWash* in 2006. (Courtesy of Michaela Chowning.)

Ellen Marie started out as an open trap net boat built in 1926. She worked in the pound-net and winter crab-dredge fisheries and, in this photograph, is still carrying a dredge post. When this photograph was taken in 2012, she was owned by Paul Vrooman and was being used for recreation. (Author's collection.)

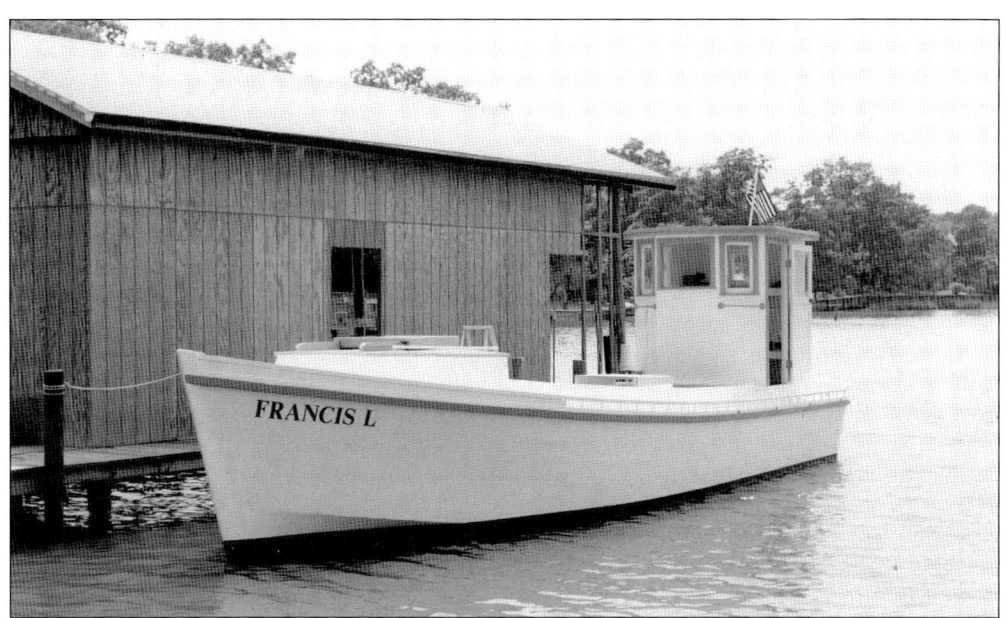

Northumberland, Virginia, boatbuilder Francis Haynie constructed *Francis L.* in 2004. This was the last Chesapeake Bay deck boat created by a traditional bay boatbuilder. Haynie selected, cut, and cured his own wood from local forest to provide timbers and planks for the boat. Although Haynie used electric tools, he often found his 19th-century boatbuilding tools to be just as efficient. The boat is named for him. (Author's collection.)

This modern forepeak hatch on *Francis L.* has a slide top-hatch and handrails on the top deck. On traditional deck boats, forepeaks provided sleeping quarters for the crew, as well as storage and ballast space. On some larger deck boats, the galley was located in the forepeak, as indicated by a stovepipe sticking out of the forepeak roof deck. (Author's collection.)

The late Francis Haynie of Heathsville, Virginia, owned and operated Haynie's Boatyard and built the last traditional Chesapeake Bay deck boat in Virginia. Haynie grew up on the Northern Neck amongst a traditional wood culture. He made canvasback decoys from red cedar, oyster nipper handles from ash, sculling paddles and oars from white oak, shad skiff knees from sassafras and catalpa, and trunnels (used to fasten log canoes together) from locust. (Author's collection.)

Winnie Estelle was built in 1920 by Noah T. Evans of Smith Island, Maryland. Evans named the boat after his two daughters. The vessel was sold and moved out of the Chesapeake Bay region in the 1960s and ended up sunk on a shoal off Belize in the Caribbean. She was salvaged and restored and used as a tour, dive, and charter boat out of San Pedro, Belize. Today, she is owned by the Chesapeake Bay Maritime Museum in St. Michaels, Maryland, and used as an education boat. (Courtesy of Kim Granberry.)

Deck boats at the 2012 Chesapeake Bay Buyboat Rendezvous are shown leaving Tangier Island in a caravan en route to J. Millard Tawes Historical Museum in Crisfield, Maryland. After Crisfield, the next stop for the group of 13 boats was Calvert Marine Museum in Solomons, then on to the Annapolis Maritime Museum in Annapolis. The group then headed to the Chester River for a visit at the home of Capt. Barry Buckley, owner of *East Hampton*, and stayed a while at Rolph's

Wharf Marina with Capt. Tom Parker of *Thomas J.* as host. The final stop on the 2012 trip was at the annual Pirate's Weekend at Rock Hall. The boats arrived in Rock Hall with cannons firing. Fifteen reunions have been held. Since the beginning, the captain of Little *Muriel Eileen*, David Cantera, and his wife, Lena, and their family have participated each year. (Author's collection.)

Ted and Mimi Parish own and maintain one of the finest deck boats on the bay. *Nellie Crockett* was built in 1925 by Crisfield boatbuilder Charles A. Dana for Andrew A. Crockett of Tangier Island. The vessel was designated a National Historic Landmark in 1994. The boat is shown arriving in Urbanna, Virginia, for the 2018 Chesapeake Bay Buyboat Rendezvous. (Author's collection.)

The annual rendezvous is not just about yachts and education boats. At the 2010 event in Urbanna, Jerry Pruitt of Tangier Island arrived in his working deck boat *Delvin K.*, which was built in 1949 by Sidney Smith of Bena, Virginia. The boat is the last buyboat in Virginia that still buys oysters from oystermen. (Author's collection.)

Peggy is perhaps the only deck boat on the bay that was converted into a yacht and then reconverted to its former workboat state. Gretchen and Kim Granberry converted *Peggy* into a yacht and attended the first buyboat rendezvous in 2004. The Granberrys later donated *Peggy* to the Mathews Maritime Foundation and Museum. The museum's boat shop crew took off the trunk cabin and other yacht features and brought the vessel back to its original state. (Author's collection.)

The survival of the small fleet of deck boats left on the bay will be a challenge. The boats are made of wood and are old. The cost of maintaining large wooden boats is expensive, and the wooden boat culture that generationally maintained the boats is disappearing. The future of the fleets rests in the hands of those who have the finances and the cultural will to maintain this dynamic part of the bay's living maritime history. (Courtesy of Hannah Straub.)

In this picture taken at the 2018 Chesapeake Bay Buyboat Rendezvous in Deltaville, Virginia, boats are jammed together at the dock at Chesapeake Boat Works on Fishing Bay. Chesapeake Boat Works is near the site of the old Deagle & Son Marine Railway, where many deck boats were built, repaired, enlarged, and converted to power. Lee Deagle and his son Ed purchased the railway in the 1930s, and prior to that, Linwood Price built boats on the site. Price and his son Milford were two of the most prolific boatbuilders on the bay. The largest deck boat ever built on the Chesapeake, *Marydel*, was built by the Prices not even a stone's throw from where the boats are moored in this photograph. (Author's collection.)

BIBLIOGRAPHY

Burgess, Robert H. *Chesapeake Circle*. Cambridge, MD: Cornell Maritime Press Inc., 1965.
———. *Chesapeake Sailing Craft, Part One*. Cambridge, MD: Tidewater Publishers, 1975.
———. *Chesapeake Sailing Craft: Recollections of Robert Burgess*. Edited by William A. Fox. Centreville, MD: Tidewater Publishers, 2005.
Chowning, Larry S. *Chesapeake Bay Buyboats*, Centreville, MD: Tidewater Publishers, 2003.
———. *Chesapeake Legacy*. Centreville, MD: Tidewater Publishers, 1995.
———. *Deadrise and Cross-planked*. Centreville, MD: Tidewater Publishers, 2007
———. *Harvesting the Chesapeake Tools and Traditions*. Centreville, MD: Tidewater Publishers, 1990.
Frye, John. *The Men All Singing the Story of Menhaden Fishing*. Virginia Beach, VA: Donning, 1978.
Johnson, Paula J., ed. *Working the Water: The Commercial Fisheries of Maryland's Patuxent River*. Charlottesville: University Press of Virginia, 1988.
Lang, Varley. *Follow The Water*. Winston-Salem, NC: John F. Blair Publisher, 1961.
Smith, Karla. *The River Bins Us: A Story by the People of Crittenden, Eclipse, and Hobson*. Suffolk, VA: Hallmark Publishing Co., 2007.

DISCOVER THOUSANDS OF LOCAL HISTORY BOOKS FEATURING MILLIONS OF VINTAGE IMAGES

Arcadia Publishing, the leading local history publisher in the United States, is committed to making history accessible and meaningful through publishing books that celebrate and preserve the heritage of America's people and places.

Find more books like this at
www.arcadiapublishing.com

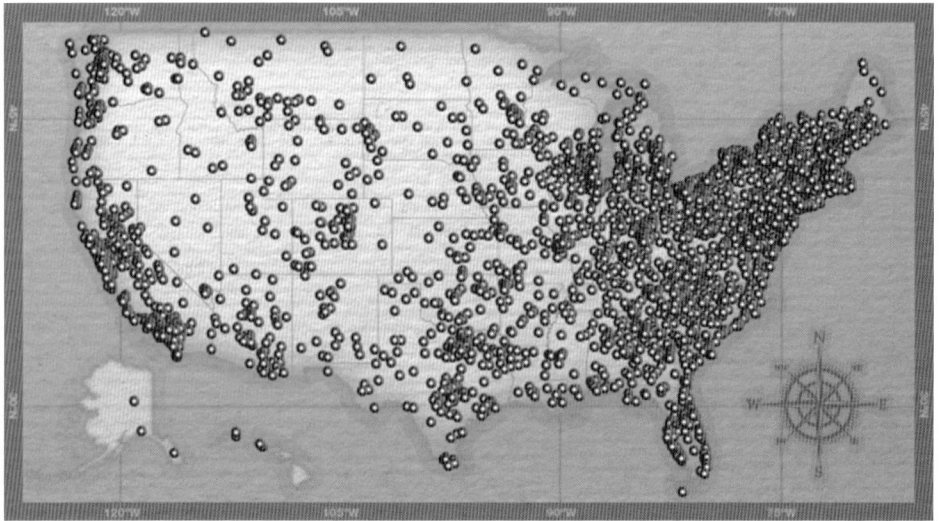

Search for your hometown history, your old stomping grounds, and even your favorite sports team.

Consistent with our mission to preserve history on a local level, this book was printed in South Carolina on American-made paper and manufactured entirely in the United States. Products carrying the accredited Forest Stewardship Council (FSC) label are printed on 100 percent FSC-certified paper.